On the *Revival of the Religious Sciences* (*Iḥyāʾ ʿulūm al-dīn*)

"The *Iḥyāʾ ʿulūm al-dīn* is the most valuable and most beautiful of books."

—Ibn Khallikān (d. 681/1282)

"The *Iḥyāʾ ʿulūm al-dīn* is one of al-Ghazālī's best works."

—Aḥmad b. ʿAbd al-Ḥalīm (d. 728/1328)

"Any seeker of [felicity of] the hereafter cannot do without the *Iḥyāʾ ʿulūm al-dīn*"

—Tāj al-Dīn al-Subkī (d. 771/1370)

"The *Iḥyāʾ ʿulūm al-dīn* is a marvelous book containing a wide variety of Islamic sciences intermixed with many subtle accounts of Sufism and matters of the heart."

—Ibn Kathīr (d. 774/1373)

"The *Iḥyāʾ ʿulūm al-dīn* is one of best and greatest books on admonition, it was said concerning it, 'if all the books of Islam were lost except for the *Iḥyāʾ* it would suffice what was lost.'"

—Ḥājjī Khalīfa Kātib Čelebī (d. 1067/1657)

"The *Iḥyāʾ* [*ʿulūm al-dīn*] is one of [Imām al-Ghazālī's] most noble works, his most famous work, and by far his greatest work'"

—Muḥammad Murtaḍā l-Zabīdī (d. 1205/1791)

On Imām al-Ghazālī

"Al-Ghazālī is [like] a deep ocean [of knowledge]."

—Imām al-Ḥaramayn al-Juwaynī (d. 478/1085)

"Al-Ghazālī is the second [Imām] Shāfiʿī."

—Muḥammad b. Yaḥyā l-Janzī (d. 549/1154)

"Abū Ḥāmid al-Ghazālī, the Proof of Islam (Ḥujjat al-Islām) and the Muslims, the Imām of the *imāms* of religion, [is a man] whose like eyes have not seen in eloquence and elucidation, and speech and thought, and acumen and natural ability."

—ʿAbd al-Ghāfir b. Ismāʿīl al-Fārisī (d. 529/1134)

"[He was] the Proof of Islam and Muslims, Imām of the imāms of religious sciences, one of vast knowledge, the wonder of the ages, the author of many works, and [a man] of extreme intelligence and the best of the sincere."

—Imām al-Dhahabī (d. 748/1347)

"Al-Ghazālī is without doubt the most remarkable figure in all Islam."

—T.J. DeBoer

". . . A man who stands on a level with Augustine and Luther in religious insight and intellectual vigor."

—H.A.R. Gibb

"I have to some extent found, and I believe others can find, in the words and example of al-Ghazālī a true *iḥyāʾ* . . ."

—Richard J. McCarthy, S.J.

ٱعْلَمُوٓا۟ أَنَّمَا ٱلْحَيَوٰةُ ٱلدُّنْيَا لَعِبٌ وَلَهْوٌ وَزِينَةٌ وَتَفَاخُرٌۢ بَيْنَكُمْ وَتَكَاثُرٌ فِى
ٱلْأَمْوَٰلِ وَٱلْأَوْلَٰدِ ۖ ﴿٢٠﴾

Know that the life of this world is but amusement, diversion, adornment, boasting to one another, and competition in increase of wealth and children...

Sūrat al-Ḥadīd

57:20

The Forty Books of the Revival of the Religious Sciences (*Iḥyāʾ ʿulūm al-dīn*)

The Quarter of Worship

1 The Book of Knowledge
2 The Principles of the Creed
3 The Mysteries of Purification
4 The Mysteries of the Prayer
5 The Mysteries of Charity
6 The Mysteries of Fasting
7 The Mysteries of the Pilgrimage
8 The Etiquette of the Recitation of the Qurʾān
9 Invocations and Supplications
10 The Arrangement of the Litanies and the Exposition of the Night Vigil

The Quarter of Customs

11 The Proprieties of Eating
12 The Proprieties of Marriage
13 The Proprieties of Acquisition and Earning a Living
14 The Lawful and the Unlawful
15 The Proprieties of Friendship and Brotherhood
16 The Proprieties of Retreat
17 The Proprieties of Travel
18 The Proprieties of the Audition and Ecstasy
19 The Commanding of Right and the Forbidding of Wrong
20 The Proprieties of Living and the Prophetic Mannerisms

The Quarter of Perils

21 The Exposition of the Wonders of the Heart
22 Training the Soul, Refining the Character, and Treating the Ailments of the Heart
23 Overcoming the Two Desires
24 The Bane of the Tongue
25 The Bane of Anger, Malice, and Envy
26 **The Censure of This World**
27 The Censure of Greed and the Love of Wealth
28 The Censure of Fame and Hypocritical Ostentation
29 The Censure of Pride and Vanity
30 The Censure of Deceit

The Quarter of Deliverance

31 On Repentance
32 On Patience and Thankfulness
33 On Fear and Hope
34 On Poverty and Abstinence
35 On Unity and Trust
36 On Love, Longing, Intimacy, and Contentment
37 On Intention, Sincerity, and Truthfulness
38 On Vigilance and Accounting
39 On Contemplation
40 On the Remembrance of Death and the Hereafter

THE CENSURE OF THIS WORLD
Kitāb dhamm al-dunyā

Book 26 of

Iḥyāʾ ʿulūm al-dīn

The Revival of the Religious Sciences

بسم الله الرحمن الرحيم

AL-GHAZĀLĪ

Kitāb dhamm al-dunyā

THE CENSURE OF THIS WORLD

Book 26 of the *Iḥyāʾ ʿulūm al-dīn*

THE REVIVAL OF THE RELIGIOUS SCIENCES

Translated *by* Matthew B. Ingalls

Fons Vitae
2023

The Censure of This World, Book 26 of *The Revival of the Religious Sciences* first published in 2023 by

Fons Vitae
49 Mockingbird Valley Drive
Louisville, KY 40207 USA

www.fonsvitae.com

The Fons Vitae Ghazali Series
Library of Congress Control Number: 2022952163
ISBN 978-1-94-1610-64-0

Copyediting and indexing: Valerie Joy Turner
Book design and typesetting: www.scholarlytype.com
Text typeface: Adobe Minion Pro 11/13.5

Cover art courtesy of National Library of Egypt, Cairo. Qurʾānic frontispiece to part 19. Written and illuminated by ʿAbdallāh b. Muḥammad al-Ḥamadānī for Sultan Uljaytu 713/1313. Hamadan.

Printed in Canada

Contents

Editor's Note

THIS is the complete translation of *Kitāb dhamm al-dunyā* (*The Censure of This World*) book 26 of the *Iḥyāʾ ʿulūm al-dīn* of Abū Ḥāmid Muḥammad al-Ghazālī. It is a translation of the published Arabic text of volume 6 (pages 7–110), edited by Dār al-Minhāj (Jedda, 2011); the Dār al-Minhāj editors utilized manuscripts and early printed editions, as mentioned on pages 51–111 of the introductory volume.

Arabic terms that appear in italics follow the transliteration system of the *International Journal of Middle East Studies*. Common era (CE) dates have been added and follow Hijri dates. The blessings on prophets and others, as used by Imām al-Ghazālī, are represented in the original Arabic, as listed below.

Arabic	English	Usage
عَزَّوَجَلَّ	Mighty and majestic is He	On mention of God
سُبْحَانَهُ وَتَعَالَىٰ	Exalted and most high is He	Used together or separately
صَلَّى ٱللَّهُ عَلَيْهِ وَسَلَّمَ	Blessings and peace of God be upon him	On mention of the Prophet Muḥammad
عَلَيْهِ ٱلسَّلَامُ	Peace be upon him	On mention of one
عَلَيْهِمُ ٱلسَّلَامُ	Peace be upon them	or more prophets
رَضِيَ ٱللَّهُ عَنْهُ	God be pleased with him	On mention of one or more
رَضِيَ ٱللَّهُ عَنْهُمْ	God be pleased with them	Companions of the Prophet
رَضِيَ ٱللَّهُ عَنْهَا	God be pleased with her	On mention of a female Companion of the Prophet
رَحِمَهُ ٱللَّهُ	God have mercy on him	On mention of someone who is deceased

This translation includes the footnotes and references provided by the editors of the Dār al-Minhāj edition. In addition, the translator has added comments and included references to Murtaḍā l-Zabīdī's *Itḥāf* (a detailed commentary on the *Iḥyāʾ ʿulūm al-dīn*) and identified many of Imām al-Ghazālī's sources. The editors have provided explanatory footnotes as necessary; these are followed by [eds.]. Editorial clarifications in the text appear in hard brackets.

In addition, we have compiled a short biography of Imām al-Ghazālī with a chronology of important events in his life. This is followed by an extract from Imām al-Ghazālī's introduction to the *Iḥyāʾ ʿulūm al-dīn;* it serves as a guide to the *Revival of the Religious Sciences* for those reading Imām al-Ghazālī for the first time. For this edition we included the page numbers of this book in volume 6 of the Arabic edition; these appear in the margins after the vertical line mark |.

Biography of Imām al-Ghazālī

He is Abū Ḥāmid Muḥammad b. Muḥammad b. Muḥammad b. Aḥmad al-Ghazālī l-Ṭūsī; he was born in 450/1058 in the village of Ṭabarān near Ṭūs (in northeast Iran) and he died there, at the age of fifty-five, in 505/1111. Muḥammad's father died when he and his younger brother Aḥmad were still young; their father left a little money for their education in the care of a Sufi friend of limited means. When the money ran out, their caretaker suggested that they enroll in a *madrasa*. The *madrasa* system meant they had a stipend, room, and board. Al-Ghazālī studied *fiqh* in his hometown under a Sufi named Aḥmad al-Rādhakānī; he then traveled to Jurjān and studied under Ismāʿīl b. Masʿada al-Ismāʿīlī (d. 477/1084).

On his journey home his caravan was overtaken by highway robbers who took all of their possessions. Al-Ghazālī went to the leader of the bandits and demanded his notebooks. The leader asked, what are these notebooks? Al-Ghazālī answered: "This is the knowledge that I traveled far to acquire," the leader acquiesced to al-Ghazālī's demands after stating: "If you claim that it is knowledge that you have, how can we take it away from you?" This incident left a lasting impression on the young scholar. Thereafter, he returned to Ṭūs for three years, where he committed to memory all that he had learned thus far.

In 469/1077 he traveled to Nīshāpūr to study with the leading scholar of his time, Imām al-Ḥaramayn al-Juwaynī (d. 478/1085), at the Niẓāmiyya College; al-Ghazālī remained his student for approximately eight years, until al-Juwaynī died. Al-Ghazālī was one of his most illustrious students, and al-Juwaynī referred to him as "a deep ocean [of knowledge]." As one of al-Juwaynī star pupils, al-Ghazālī used to fill in as a substitute lecturer in his teacher's absence. He also tutored his fellow students in the subjects that al-Juwaynī taught at the Niẓāmiyya. Al-Ghazālī wrote his first book, on the founding principles of legal theory (*uṣūl al-fiqh*), while studying with al-Juwaynī.

Very little is known about al-Ghazālī's family, though some biographers mention that he married while in Nīshāpūr; others note that he had married in Ṭūs prior to leaving for Nīshāpūr. Some accounts state that he had five children, a son who died early and four daughters. Accounts also indicate that his mother lived to see her son rise to fame and fortune.

After the death of al-Juwaynī, al-Ghazālī went to the camp (*al-muʿaskar*) of the Saljūq *wazīr* Niẓām al-Mulk (d. 485/1192). He stayed at the camp, which was a gathering place for scholars, and quickly distinguished himself among their illustrious company. Niẓām al-Mulk recognized al-Ghazālī's genius and appointed him professor at the famed Niẓāmiyya College of Baghdad.

Al-Ghazālī left for Baghdad in 484/1091 and stayed there four years—it was a very exciting time to be in the heart of the Islamic empire. At the Niẓāmiyya College he had many students, by some estimates as many as three hundred. In terms of his scholarly output, this was also a prolific period in which he wrote *Maqāṣid al-falāsifa, Tahāfut al-falāsifa, al-Mustaẓhirī,* and other works.

Al-Ghazālī was well-connected politically and socially; we have evidence that he settled disputes related to the legitimacy of the rule of the ʿAbbāsid caliph, al-Mustaẓhir (r. 487–512/1094–1118) who assumed his role as the caliph when he was just fifteen years old, after the death of his father al-Muqtadī (d. 487/1094). Al-Ghazālī issued a *fatwā* of approval of the appointment of al-Mustaẓhir and was present at the oath-taking ceremony.

In Baghdad, al-Ghazālī underwent a spiritual crisis, during which he was overcome by fear of the punishment of the hellfire. He became convinced that he was destined for the hellfire if he did not change his ways; he feared that he had become too engrossed in worldly affairs, to the detriment of his spiritual being. He began to question his true intentions: was he writing and teaching to serve God, or because he enjoyed the fame and fortune that resulted from his lectures. He experienced much suffering, both inward and outward; one day as he stood before his students to present a lecture, he found himself unable to speak. The physicians were unable to diagnose any physical malady. Al-Ghazālī remained in Baghdad for a time, then left his teaching post for the pilgrimage. He left behind fortune, fame, and influence. He was beloved by his numerous students and had many admirers, including the sultan; he was also envied by many. The presumption is that he left in the manner he did—ostensibly to undertake the pilgrimage—because if he had made public his intentions to leave permanently, those around him would have tried to convince him to remain and the temptation might have been too strong to resist.

After leaving Baghdad, he changed direction and headed toward Damascus; according to his autobiography he disappeared from the intellectual scene for ten years. This does not mean that he did not teach, but that he did not want to return to public life and be paid for teaching. This ten-year period can be divided into two phases. First, he spent two years in the East—in greater Syria and on the pilgrimage. We have evidence that while on his return to Ṭūs he appeared at a Sufi lodge opposite the Niẓāmiyya College in Baghdad. He spent the second phase of the ten-year period (the remaining eight years) in Ṭūs, where he wrote the famed *Iḥyāʾ ʿulūm al-dīn*, a work that was inspired by the change in his outlook that resulted from his spiritual crisis.

When he arrived back in his hometown in 490/1097, he established a school and a Sufi lodge, in order to continue teaching and learning. In 499/1106, Niẓām al-Mulk's son, Fakhr al-Mulk, requested that al-Ghazālī accept a teaching position at his old school, the Niẓāmiyya of Nīshāpūr. He accepted and taught for a time, but left this position in 500/1106 after Fakhr al-Mulk was assassinated by Ismāʿīlīs. He then returned to Ṭūs and divided his time between teaching and worship. He died in 505/1111 and was buried in a cemetery near the citadel of Ṭābarān.

Legacy and Contributions of al-Ghazālī

Al-Ghazālī's two hundred and seventy-three works span many disciplines and can be grouped under the following headings.

1. Jurisprudence and legal theory. Al-Ghazālī made foundational contributions to Shāfiʿī jurisprudence; his book *al-Wajīz* is major handbook that has been used in teaching institutions around the world; many commentaries have been written on it, most notably by Abū l-Qāsim ʿAbd al-Karīm al-Rāfiʿī (d. 623/1226). In legal theory, *al-Mustaṣfa min ʿilm al-uṣūl* is considered one of five foundational texts in the discipline.
2. Logic and philosophy. Al-Ghazālī introduced logic in Islamic terms that jurists could understand and utilize. His works on philosophy include the *Tahāfut al-falāsifa*, which has been studied far beyond the Muslim world and has been the subject of numerous commentaries, discussions, and refutations.
3. Theology, including works on heresiography in refutation of Bāṭinī doctrines. He also expounded on the theory of occasionalism.
4. Ethics and educational theory. The *Mīzān al-ʿamal* and other works such as the *Iḥyāʾ ʿulūm al-dīn* mention a great deal on education.
5. Spirituality and Sufism. His magnum opus, the *Iḥyāʾ ʿulūm al-dīn* is a pioneering work in the field of spirituality, in terms of its organization and its comprehensive scope.
6. Various fields. Al-Ghazālī also wrote shorter works in a variety of disciplines, including his autobiography (*al-Munqidh min al-ḍalāl*), works on Qurʾānic studies (*Jawāhir al-Qurʾān*), and political statecraft (*Naṣiḥat al-mūluk*).

Chronology of al-Ghazālī's Life

450/1058	Birth of al-Ghazālī at Ṭūs
c. 461/1069	Began studies at Ṭūs
c. 465/1073	Traveled to Jurjān to study
466–469/1074–1077	Studied at Ṭūs
469/1077	Studied with al-Jūwaynī at the Niẓāmiyya college in Nīshāpūr
473/1080	al-Ghazālī composed his first book, *al-Mankhūl fī l-uṣūl*
477/1084	Death of al-Fāramdhī, one of al-Ghazālī's teachers
25 Rabīʿ II 478/ 20 August 1085	Death of al-Jūwaynī; al-Ghazālī left Nīshāpūr
Jumāda I 484/ July 1091	Appointed to teach at the Niẓāmiyya college in Baghdad
10 Ramaḍān 485/ 14 October 1092	Niẓām-al-Mulk was assassinated
484–487/1091–1094	Studied philosophy
Muḥarrām 487/ February 1094	Attended the oath-taking of the new caliph, al-Mustaẓhir
487/1094	Finished *Maqāṣid al-falāsifa*
5 Muḥarrām 488/ 21 January 1095	Finished *Tahāfut al-falāsifa*
Rajab 488/ July 1095	Experienced a spiritual crisis
Dhū l-Qaʿda 488/ November 1095	Left Baghdad for Damascus
Dhū l-Qaʿda 489/ November – December 1096	Made pilgrimage and worked on the *Iḥyāʾ ʿulūm al-dīn*
Jumāda II 490/ May 1097	Taught from the *Iḥyāʾ ʿulūm al-dīn* during a brief stop in Baghdad
Rajab 490/June 1097	Seen in Baghdad by Abū Bakr b. al-ʿArabī
Fall 490/1097	Returned to Ṭūs

Dhū l-Ḥijja 490/ November 1097	Established a *madrasa* and a *khānqāh* in Ṭūs
Dhū l-Qaʿda 499/ July 1106	Taught at the Niẓāmiyya college in Nīshāpūr
500/1106	Wrote *al-Munqidh min al-ḍalāl*
500/1106	Returned to Ṭūs
28 Dhū l-Ḥijja 502/ 5 August 1109	Finished *al-Mustaṣfā min ʿilm al-uṣūl*
Jumada I 505/ December 1111	Finished *Iljām al-ʿawām ʿan ʿilm al-kalām*
14 Jumada II 505/ 18 December 1111	Imām al-Ghazālī died in Ṭūs

Eulogies in Verse

Because of him the lame walked briskly,
And the songless through him burst into melody.

On the death of Imām al-Ghazālī, Abū l-Muẓaffar Muḥammad al-Abiwardī said of his loss:

He is gone! and the greatest loss which ever afflicted me,
was that of a man who left no one like him among mankind.

About the *Revival of the Religious Sciences*

THE present work is book 16 of Imām al-Ghazālī's forty-volume masterpiece. Below is an excerpt from al-Ghazālī's introduction that explains the arrangement and purpose of the *Iḥyāʾ ʿulūm al-dīn*.

People have composed books concerning some of these ideas, but this book [the *Iḥyāʾ*] differs from them in five ways, by

1. clarifying what they have obscured and elucidating what they have treated casually;
2. arranging what they scattered and putting in order what they separated;
3. abbreviating what they made lengthy and proving what they reported;
4. omitting what they have repeated; and
5. establishing the truth of certain obscure matters that are difficult to understand and which have not been presented in books at all.

For although all the scholars follow one course, there is no reason one should not proceed independently and bring to light something unknown, paying special attention to something his colleagues have forgotten. Or they are not heedless about calling attention to it, but they neglect to mention it in books. Or they do not overlook it, but something prevents them from exposing it [and making it clear].

So these are the special properties of this book, besides its inclusion of all these various kinds of knowledge.

Two things induced me to arrange this book in four parts. The first and fundamental motive is that this arrangement in establishing what is true and in making it understandable is, as it were, inevitable because the branch of knowledge by which one approaches the hereafter is divided into the knowledge of [proper] conduct and the knowledge of [spiritual] unveiling.

By the knowledge of [spiritual] unveiling I mean knowledge and only knowledge. By the science of [proper] conduct I mean knowledge as well as action in accordance with that knowledge. This work will deal only with the science of [proper] conduct, and not with [spiritual] unveiling, which one is not permitted to record in writing, although it is the ultimate aim of saints and the ultimate aim of the sincere. The science of [proper] conduct is merely a path that leads to unveiling and only through that path did the prophets of God communicate with the people and lead them to Him. Concerning [spiritual] unveiling, the prophets عَلَيْهِمُ السَّلَامُ spoke only figuratively and briefly through signs and symbols, because they realized the inability of people's minds to comprehend. Therefore since the scholars are heirs of the prophets, they cannot but follow in their footsteps and emulate their way.

The knowledge of [proper] conduct is divided into (1) outward knowledge, by which I mean knowledge of the senses and (2) inward knowledge, by which I mean knowledge of the functions of the heart.

The physical members either perform acts of prescribed worship, or acts that are in accordance with custom, while the heart, because it is removed from the senses and belongs to the world of dominion, is subject to either praiseworthy or blameworthy [influences]. Therefore it is necessary to divide this branch of knowledge into two parts: outward and inward. The outward part, which is connected to the senses, is subdivided into acts of worship and acts that pertain to custom. The inward part, which is connected to the states of the heart and the characteristics of the soul, is subdivided into blameworthy states and praiseworthy states. So the total makes four divisions of the sciences of the practice of religion.

The second motive [for this division] is that I have noticed the sincere interest of students in jurisprudence, which has become popular among those who do not fear God تَعَالَىٰ but who seek to boast and exploit its influence and prestige in arguments. It [jurisprudence] is also divided into four quarters, and he who follows the style of one who is beloved becomes beloved.

Translator's Introduction

In the twenty-sixth book of *The Revival of the Religious Sciences* (*Iḥyāʾ ʿulūm al-dīn*), *The Book of the Censure of This World* (*Kitāb Dhamm al-dunyā*), Abū Ḥāmid Muḥammad b. Muḥammad al-Ghazālī (d. 505/1111) condemns this world. He reveals its evils and the ways in which it entraps people, causing them to lose their hereafter. Al-Ghazālī then focuses his rhetoric on the correct attitude a Muslim should hold toward this world. He presents the dilemma of how one can live in this world, but not let it overwhelm one's heart; how one can properly understand his own relation to this world and work and interact in it, but in a way that is not *of* this world, but for one's hereafter.

The life of this world (*al-ḥayātu al-dunyā*), or this world (*al-dunyā*) derives from the Arabic word for proximity (*dunūw*). The term indicates "the nearest abode" at hand. Its opposite is the hereafter (*al-ākhira*), which more literally signifies "the last," as it is the last abode of human existence. The etymology of *dunyā* also imbues the term with connotations of lowliness and baseness, which is confirmed in the Qurʾān.[1] Although it is not synonymous with the earth (*al-arḍ*) per se, according to the author, *al-dunyā* encompasses everything in the realm of what is seen (*ʿālam al-shahāda*); interestingly, al-Ghazālī's later analysis notes that some actions, if undertaken with an eye toward the hereafter, are not of this world.

The Censure of This World comprises a brief introduction and five chapters. The first chapter includes primary source texts—reports (*akhbār*), traditions (*āthār*), and longer exhortations (*mawāʿiẓ*)—that warn reader of the dangers and evils of this world. Al-Ghazālī allows these texts to speak for themselves and adds very little commentary to them. His second chapter presents examples of this

1 See, inter alia, Q. 87:16: *But you prefer the life of this world.*

world to illustrate its true nature. A third chapter contains the crux of al-Ghazālī's thought about this world; in it he explains why it is condemned and what should be included and excluded from the definition of this world. A fourth chapter analyzes this world from an almost sociological perspective; it enumerates why people need others and the ways in which they must come together to provide the necessities of life; it then identifies the essential occupations and the aspects of society that flow from them.

The first chapter of *The Censure of This World* cites *ḥadīth*s of the Prophet Muḥammad and reports from the prophets Jesus,[2] Moses, Adam, Solomon, Abraham, and Noah, along with a long exhortation by the Companion Abū l-Dardāʾ (d. 32/652 or 653). From these texts, in addition to a rhymed couplet of poetry, we learn that this world is "cursed," that it is "the beginning of every misdeed," the most odious thing to God, and the cause of destruction and damnation for people who are otherwise pious. Moreover, this world is bewitching and duplicitous, while it consumes the faith and overwhelms the minds of believers. Chapter 1 also comprises traditions (*āthār*) and excerpts of poetry that communicate similar attitudes toward this world. These passages have a common theme; namely, that this world and the hereafter cannot coexist in a single heart.

In the second chapter, some of the longer exhortations, or admonitions (*mawāʿiẓ*), in condemnation of this world were originally delivered as sermons (sing. *khuṭba*). These longer passages include themes such as the inevitability of death, the ways this world wears one down and deceives, and the ways that wise people work for their eternal abode while foolish people fail to do so. Al-Ghazālī's source for this material seems to be from the books *Dhamm al-dunyā* (The censure of this world) and *Kitāb al-zuhd* (The book of renunciation) of ʿAbdallāh Ibn Abī l-Dunyā (d. 281/894), and the *Ḥilyat al-awliyāʾ* (The ornament of the saints) of Abū Nuʿaym al-Iṣbahānī (d. 430/1038), books which were available in his time.

2 For help in understanding why Jesus would be quoted so heavily, see Khalidi, *The Muslim Jesus*.

The third chapter of *The Censure of This World* ("An elucidation of the character of this world through examples") presents examples of this world that al-Ghazālī derived from an array of sources, including *ḥadīth*s, poetry, and his own inspiration. A few of these examples are introduced through a single *ḥadīth* text or tradition with no further commentary, while for others the author expands on the symbolism. In some of these examples, water plays a central role: It is an obstacle in people's way, and in their attempts to traverse it (by bridge, boat, or foot) they expose themselves to dangers that are analogous to the dangers of this world.

In other examples, a crone represents this world: She uses her many adornments to conceal her true form and deceive her suitors, and later she slays these same suitors or summons them to hell. In this manner, she herself symbolizes *al-dunyā*—a feminine word in Arabic that allows al-Ghazālī to transition creatively between the symbol and the thing symbolized. Though descriptions of the crone as blind, decrepit, and (usually) toothless serve to emphasize her ugliness, they also reinforce her essential deceitfulness, as presumably such qualities would render her less threatening, though in fact she is a dangerous foe who lies in wait to ambush her prey.

Notably, al-Ghazālī uses food and excrement as symbols to highlight the nature of worldly pleasures. Just as food inevitably becomes something revolting and noxious, so too do worldly pleasures, which ultimately burden one with the anguish of separation at the time of death and a prolonged reckoning in the hereafter. Al-Ghazālī uses the example of excrement because its foulness is inversely proportional to the deliciousness of the food that it once was.

The burden of worldly possessions and delights figures prominently in the longest of al-Ghazālī's examples, which tells a parable of a ship that lands on a desert island. In this parable, the captain allows the passengers to disembark, but issues strict orders to return promptly before the ship departs. The tale of these passengers, who obey or disobey the captain in various degrees, is a lesson on the human condition, which is more often than not overwhelmed by greed and tricked by the temptations of worldly attractions. Thus, the ship symbolizes the passage of life, and though al-Ghazālī does not emphasize it, the ship's captain would seem to personify a prophetic figure who warns of the ship's imminent departure and calls out to the wandering passengers. The island's dazzling sights, sounds, smells, and curiosities represent the temptations of this world that ensnare and destroy most people.

Having thus communicated the dangers of this world to his reader through parables and primary source texts, al-Ghazālī then undertakes a discussion of the definition of this world and the connection between necessities (*ḍarūrāt*) and the complex human society around us that stems from these.

In chapter 4 of *The Censure of This World* ("An elucidation of the reality and essence of this world regarding the servant"), al-Ghazālī presents the crux of his philosophy on *al-dunyā*—a term that is relative to the individual and the intention that inspires his or her acts. Though it may seem counterintuitive to a modern reader, possession or ownership of material things is not essential to al-Ghazālī's conception of worldliness. Rather, he focuses on the enjoyment of luxuries, "by hearing a bird's song, or gazing on greenery, or sipping cool water" [p. 69], by which he clarifies his understanding of self-indulgence in this world. For al-Ghazālī, worldliness transcends social class; both rich and poor are prone to worldly self-indulgence to the detriment of their souls, whether or not they own material things or even in instances in which nothing unlawful has occurred.

Al-Ghazālī justifies his definition of worldliness by first explaining his understanding of the purpose of life in its most basic sense. In this context, he says that an individual only takes five things with him to the hereafter; therefore, the purpose of life is to cultivate these five things: knowledge of God that is gathered for His sake, acts of worship done for Him, a heart that has been purified of the desires of this world, intimacy with the remembrance of God, and love of God. To gather the first, perform the second, and imbue one's self with the latter three characteristics, a person requires food, clothing, and shelter. If a person consumes the minimum amount—what is absolutely necessary—of these three things, and he or she does so for the sake of God, in pursuit of the five things that remain after death, then he or she has not engaged with *al-dunyā* in the negative and detrimental sense of the term.

In the fifth chapter, entitled "An elucidation of the essence of the world," al-Ghazālī illustrates how the human need for food, clothing, and shelter leads to the numerous occupations and trades that form the complex society in which we live. According to al-Ghazālī, humans must come together to procreate, cooperate in raising children, and manage the division of labor that provides food, clothing, and security against external threats. These basic needs give rise to five fundamental occupations: farming, herding, hunting, weaving, and construction. These, along with the corollary trades of carpentry, metalsmithing, and leatherworking, form the first foundational type of occupations. To protect laborers from external threats such as raiders and thieves, and from internecine conflict such as disputes over resources and property, a second type of professions emerged, chief among these is soldiering. Because this second type cannot generate a livelihood without neglecting its responsibilities, the need arises for taxes to transfer wealth from the first profession to another. This in turn gives rise to a third type, that of administrators, tax collectors and assessors, treasurers, and so on.

This integrated system of occupations and professions requires people to be unified in a political organization, at the head of which sits a sovereign to govern. To match the needs of people across space and time, the system also requires specialized professions (e.g., to manage markets and storehouses, transport goods, etc.), a durable currency, and the means to assess value when exchanging these goods. Finally, the system assumes a high degree of training and skills on the part of its participants, while those who neglect this training in their youth, or who experience disability, end up relying on the work of others for their livelihood. According to al-Ghazālī, this in turn generates the occupations (or professions) of thievery, which has types such as highwaymen, beggars, street performers, and charlatans.

As noted, the complexity of this integrated system of human occupations distracts most people and causes them to lose sight of their true purpose in life and how to lead their lives. Al-Ghazālī provides examples of five erroneous approaches: first, those who work to eat and eat to work. Those locked in this binary system of short-sighted purpose never consider the larger meaning behind their existence until the time comes to leave this world. A second approach is that of the hedonists whose purpose is to gratify their desires for food and sex. A third approach is explained as those whose focus is on acquiring as much wealth and treasure as possible in this life, while consuming as little as possible. Though a person may ultimately toil and acquire a sizeable fortune, it serves only as a source of pleasure for the one who consumes it, usually a relative who inherits it or a despot who seizes it. A fourth approach is taken by those who seek status and the praise of others; they strive for this world to spend it on appearances. Finally, a fifth approach is that of the sovereigns whose purpose is the attainment of status and power; they seek this by subjugating others to their will.

Al-Ghazālī devotes the rest of chapter 5 to those people who have recognized the futility of chasing after this world, but who are mistaken in how best to live in it. Such people include those who join strange suicide cults; extreme ascetics who harm themselves to the point of death or madness; and antinomians who abandon the dictates of Islamic law out of the conviction that they have transcended it or out of frustration with their earlier practices of extreme asceticism. Al-Ghazālī then elucidates his view that the correct path through life is to follow the practices of the Prophet and his Companions, as this is the middle course between extremes.

Al-Ghazālī's creativity is on full display in chapters 4 and 5 of *The Censure of This World*; indeed, these chapters may leave readers both shaken and inspired. The author's concluding remarks on the deviant approaches to this life suggest that he seeks to persuade readers to abandon worldliness to one degree or another. He persuades readers of the dangers of this world, then analyzes the simultaneous need people have to live among others. It would be reasonable to conclude that al-Ghazālī intended his *Censure of This World* as a corrective text to offset the worldly immoderation of his own generation and that of his later readers. In other words, extreme worldliness demands an equally extreme antidote, and al-Ghazālī's text functions as such an antidote, to jolt readers out of complacency.

A Final Note on the Translation

In the English translation that follows I aimed to strike a balance between clarity, eloquence, consistency of usage, and fidelity to the original Arabic text. Naturally, it comes up short here and there in balancing these variables, though I have taken fidelity to al-Ghazālī's intended meanings as my starting point and made all other variables subservient to this. After fidelity to the Arabic text, I prioritized clarity of English, even when that came at the expense of eloquence, beauty, and concision. My translation is not literal per se, though I did not shy away from literalism at times, if it proved to be the best means of communicating the author's intended meanings. Finally, I strove to maintain the consistency of my usage of terms so that non-Arabic speakers could benefit from a translation that closely maps onto the original Arabic text. That said, if the consistency of terms undermined the author's intended meanings in any way, I saw no problem in abandoning it.

It is my hope that the translation that follows will be of interest and use to all English readers, be they Muslims or non-Muslims with backgrounds in other religious or secular traditions. Although al-Ghazālī clearly envisioned a Muslim readership for *The Censure of This World*, it encompasses many ideas and arguments that I am confident will be of value, in one form or another, for all people.

THE CENSURE OF THIS WORLD

Kitāb dhamm al-dunyā

the Sixth Book of
the Quarter of
Perils
Book 26
of the *Revival of
the Religious Sciences*

[al-Ghazālī's Introduction]

9

The Book of the Censure of This World

In the Name of God, the Merciful and Compassionate

PRAISE be to God, who apprised His saints of the calamities and perils of this world and disclosed its faults and deficiencies to them until they examined its proofs and signs and weighed its merits against its evils. Then they came to know that what is objectionable about it exceeds what is good. Its hopes do not make up for its dangers, while its radiance cannot escape its own eclipse. It is in the form of an elegant woman who attracts people with her beauty, while she has ugly devious mysteries that destroy those who desire to be with her.

Furthermore, [this world] is a fugitive from those who seek it, a miser with its attention. When it does give attention, there is no safety from its evil and harms. Were it to act kindly for an hour, it would do harm for a year. Were it to do harm once, it would make this its custom, and then the calamities that accompany its attention would circle about in close succession. The commerce of its children is unprofitable and futile. Its perils are continuously pelted at the breasts of its seekers. Its vicissitudes speak to the baseness of those who seek it, for everyone who exalts in it becomes base in the end, and everyone who acts proudly because of it is on a journey toward regret.

Its nature is to flee from the one who seeks it and seek the one who flees from it. It slips away from the one who would serve it and is obliging toward the one who would shun it. Its purest portion is never free from the stains of muddiness; happiness in it is never detached from disturbances. Well-being in it gives way to sickness,

10 youthfulness in it is ceded to | decrepitude, and comfort in it results in nothing but grief and regret.

[This world] is thus a grifter and an imposter, fleeting and fleeing, continuously beautifying itself for its seekers so that, once they become enamored with it, it bares its fangs to them. It confounds them in the arrangement of the means to its ends, it discloses to them what is concealed of its wonders, and then it lets them taste its deadly poison while pelting them with its precision arrows.

Just as those who are adherents of [this world] find happiness and favor from it, it would suddenly shun them as if it were all muddled dreams. It would then bear down on them with its calamities, crushing them like harvested crops and burying them under the ground in their death shrouds. Were one of them to own all that the sun shines on, [this world] would mow it down as if it had never grown.[1] It gives its adherents hope of happiness and deceives them in its promise so that their expectations multiply, and they construct palaces. Their palaces then become graves, their amassing [of it] becomes futile, their endeavoring becomes scattered dust, and their supplications become a call for destruction.[2] This is the state of [this world]. *And ever is the command of God a destiny decreed* [Q. 33:38].

May [God's] blessings be upon Muḥammad, His servant and messenger, who was sent to all the worlds *as a bringer of good tidings and a warner* [Q. 34:28] *and an illuminating lamp* [Q. 33:46]. And may [God's blessings] be on those of his family and his Companions who assisted him in this *dīn* and supported him against the oppressors. Abundant peace be on them all.

To proceed…

This world is an enemy to God, an enemy to God's saints, and
11 an enemy to God's enemies. |

As for its enmity toward God, it [this world] has waylaid God's servants, and for this God has not looked at it [this world] since its creation.[3]

As for its enmity toward God's saints, it [this world] has beautified (*tazayyanat*) itself for them with its adornments and has encompassed

1 Lit., as if it were wealthy just yesterday.

2 Cf. Q. 25:13: …*They will cry out thereupon for destruction.*

3 This is an allusion *ḥadīth*; see p. 8, n. 14.

them with its splendor and radiance to the point that they swallowed bitter patience while disassociating themselves from it.

As for its enmity toward God's enemies, this world has gradually lured them to destruction through its deception and ruse. It has ensnared them in its net until they put their confidence in it and came to depend on it. Then it [this world] abandoned them in their utmost need, and so they reaped from it an affliction that hacks livers to pieces.[4] Moreover, it deprived them of eternal felicity (*saʿāda*), and so they grieve over their departure from it, calling out for help from its machinations, though they are not helped. Rather, it is said to them, *Remain despised therein and do not speak to Me* [Q. 23:108]; *those are the ones who have bought the life of this world in exchange for the Hereafter, so the torment will not be lightened for them, nor will they be aided* [Q. 2:86].

Since the calamities and evils of this world are tremendous, it is first necessary to recognize the reality of this world: What is it? What wisdom is there in creating it along with its enmity [toward us]? What are the entrances leading to its deceptions and evils? For whoever does not recognize evil does not protect himself from it and will fall into it.

[Below] we discuss the censure of this world, its examples, its reality, the details of its meanings, the types of occupations (*ashghāl*) connected to it, aspects of the need for foundations, and the reason people turn away from God when distracted with their excesses. If God تَعَالَىٰ so wills. And He is the one who aids in all that pleases Him.

4 Here, "an afflication that hacks livers to pieces" is a literal translation that may mean a grief that seems to have no end and no purpose.

1

An Elucidation of the Censure of This World

12

THE [Qurʾānic] verses mentioning the censure this world or similar examples are numerous. Most of the Qurʾān comprises the censure of this world, turning people away from it, and calling them to the hereafter. In fact, this is the purpose of the prophets (peace and blessings on them); they were sent only for that.

There is no need then to cite verses of the Qurʾān that are evident. We will only mention some of the reports on the matter.

It has been related that the Messenger of God ﷺ passed by a dead sheep and said, "Do you think this sheep is of little value to its owners?" [The Companions] replied, "They threw it away on account of its insignificance." He said, "By Him in whose hand is my soul! This world is less significant to God تعالى than this sheep is to its owners. If this world were equal to a gnat's wing in God's estimation, He would not give a sip of water from it to a disbeliever."[1]

And he ﷺ said, "This world is the believer's prison and the disbeliever's heaven."[2] |

13

1 Al-Tirmidhī, *Sunan*, 4:560 (nos. 2320 and 2321); Ibn Mājah, *Sunan*, 2:1376–1377 (nos. 4110 and 4111). The even-numbered *ḥadīth*s of al-Tirmidhī and Ibn Mājah are reported on the authority of al-Mustawrid b. Shaddād رضي الله عنه, while the odd-numbered *ḥadīth*s are reported on the authority of Sahl b. Saʿd رضي الله عنه.

2 Muslim, *Ṣaḥīḥ*, 4:2272 (no. 2956).

The Messenger of God صَلَّى ٱللَّهُ عَلَيْهِ وَسَلَّمَ said, "This world is cursed. What is in it is cursed except for what [is dedicated] to God."[3]

Abū Mūsā al-Ashʿarī said, "The Messenger of God صَلَّى ٱللَّهُ عَلَيْهِ وَسَلَّمَ said, 'Whoever loves his worldly [life] (*dunyāhu*) harms his hereafter, and whoever loves his hereafter harms his worldly [life]. So choose what is enduring over what is fleeting.'"[4]

And he صَلَّى ٱللَّهُ عَلَيْهِ وَسَلَّمَ said, "Love of this world is the beginning of every misdeed."[5]

Zayd b. Arqam said,

> We were with Abū Bakr al-Ṣiddīq رَضِيَ ٱللَّهُ عَنْهُ, and he asked for some water, so he was brought water with honey. When he raised it to his mouth, he wept and wept until he brought his companions to tears. They went silent but he did not, and he then started weeping again to the point that they did not think that they could bring themselves to ask him about the matter.
>
> [Zayd] continued, Then he wiped his eyes, so they asked, "Vicegerent of God's Messenger, what made you weep?"
>
> [Abū Bakr] replied, "I was with the Messenger of God صَلَّى ٱللَّهُ عَلَيْهِ وَسَلَّمَ when I saw him pushing something away from himself, though I did not see anyone with him."
>
> So I [Zayd] asked, "Messenger of God, what are you pushing away from yourself?"
>
> He said, "This world presented itself to me, so I told it, 'Get away from me!' Then it returned and said, 'Even if you escape from me, those who come after you will not.'"[6] |

14

---

3 Al-Tirmidhī, *Sunan*, 4:561 (no. 2322); Ibn Mājah, *Sunan*, 2:1377 (no. 4112). In both versions cited here, the last part (except for what belongs to God) is replaced with the words, "except for the remembrance of God, whatever assists in that, a knowledgeable person, or a person who is learning."

4 Ibn Ḥanbal, *Musnad*, 32:470 (no. 19697); Ibn Bālabān, *Musnad*, 2:486 (no. 709); al-Ḥākim al-Nīsābūrī, *al-Mustadrak*, 4:308.

5 Ibn Abī l-Dunyā, *Dhamm al-dunyā*, 16 (no. 9).

6 Ibn Abī l-Dunyā, *Dhamm al-dunyā*, 17–18 (no. 11); al-Ḥākim al-Nīsābūrī, *al-Mustadrak*, 4:309; al-Bayhaqī, *Shuʿab al-īmān*, 13:113–114 (no. 10039). Cf. al-Bazzār, *Musnad al-Bazzār*, 1:106 (no. 44).

[The Prophet] صَلَّى ٱللَّٰهُ عَلَيْهِ وَسَلَّمَ said, "How strange indeed is the [one who] believes in the abode of perpetuity and yet strives for the abode of deception!"[7]

It has been related that the Messenger of God صَلَّى ٱللَّٰهُ عَلَيْهِ وَسَلَّمَ stopped at a dunghill and said, "Step right up to this world!" He took some rags that had decomposed on that dunghill and some bones that had decayed and said, "This is this world."[8] This is an indication that the beauty of this world will wear out like those rags and the bodies that you see wearing them will become decomposed bones.

[The Prophet] صَلَّى ٱللَّٰهُ عَلَيْهِ وَسَلَّمَ said, "This world is sweet and luscious, and verily God [will] make you His successors in it and then watch how you behave. When this world was presented to the children of Israel and [the way] made accessible to them, they lost themselves in ornamentation, women, fragrance, and clothing."[9]

Jesus عَلَيْهِ ٱلسَّلَامُ said, "Do not take this world as a master lest the world take you as a slave. Store your treasure with the One who will never lose it, for the one who possesses a treasure of this world fears peril for it, while the one who possesses a treasure with God fears no such peril."[10] | 15

And [Jesus] عَلَيْهِ ٱلسَّلَامُ said,

> Oh you disciples! I have thrown this world down on its face before you, so do not raise it up after me. For part of this world's wickedness is that God is disobeyed in it, and part of this world's wickedness is that it is only by relinquishing it that the hereafter is attained. So traverse this world, and do not build it up. And know that the root of every misdeed is love of this world, while many a desire has left its possessors with long-lasting sadness.[11]

---

7 Ibn Abī Shayba, *al-Muṣannaf*, 19:89 (no. 35503); Ibn Abī l-Dunyā, *Dhamm al-dunyā*, 19 (no. 14). Cf. al-Bayhaqī, *Shuʿab al-īmān*, 13:124 (no. 10056). All are reported on the authority of Abū Jaʿfar.

8 Ibn Abī l-Dunyā, *Dhamm al-dunyā*, 21 (no. 19); al-Bayhaqī, *Shuʿab al-īmān*, 13:82 (no. 9988). The *ḥadīth* was reported on the authority of Abū Maymūn al-Lakhmī.

9 Ibn Abī l-Dunyā, *Dhamm al-dunyā*, 21–22 (no. 20), on the authority of Ḥasan; cf. Muslim, *Ṣaḥīḥ*, 4:2098 (no. 2742), on the authority of Abū Saʿīd al-Khudrī رَضِيَ ٱللَّٰهُ عَنْهُ.

10 Ibn Abī l-Dunyā, *Dhamm al-dunyā*, 25–26 (no. 31).

11 Ibn Abī l-Dunyā, *Dhamm al-dunyā*, 26 (no. 33); cf. Abū Nuʿaym, *Ḥilya*, 8:145.

[Jesus] عَلَيۡهِ ٱلسَّلَامُ also said,

> I have thrown this world down before you, and you sat on its back, so no one will contend with you over it except for kings and women. As for kings, do not contend with them over this world, for they will not concern themselves with you as long as you leave them and their worldly possessions alone. As for women, protect [yourselves] from them with fasting and prayer.[12]

[Jesus] عَلَيۡهِ ٱلسَّلَامُ also said, "This world is a seeker and is sought. This world seeks the seekers of the hereafter so it [this world] can provide his sustenance in full, while the hereafter seeks the seeker of this world until death comes to seize him by the throat."[13]

16 Mūsā b. Yasār said, "The Prophet صَلَّى ٱللَّهُ عَلَيۡهِ وَسَلَّمَ said, 'God, lofty | be His praise, has created nothing more loathesome to Him than this world, and since its creation He has not looked at it.'"[14]

It has been related that Solomon, son of David عَلَيۡهِمَا ٱلسَّلَامُ, was moving in his procession, the birds were shading him, and jinn and humans were on his right and left. [The narrator] said,

> He passed by a worshiper from the children of Israel who said, "By God, oh son of David! God has given you a tremendous kingdom!"
>
> [The narrator] said, "Solomon heard this and replied, 'One glorification of God in the believer's book of deeds is better than all that was given to the son of David, for everything that was given to the son of David will go, while the glorification of God will remain.'"[15]

---

12 Ibn Abī l-Dunyā, *Dhamm al-dunyā*, 26–27 (no. 34); al-Dīnawarī, *al-Majālisa wa-jawāhir al-ʿilm*, 170 (no. 984).

13 Ibn Abī l-Dunyā, *Dhamm al-dunyā*, 27 (no. 35); cf. al-Ṭabarānī, *al-Muʿjam al-kabīr*, 10:201 (no. 10328). Al-Ṭabarānī's narration is reported on the authority of Ibn Masʿūd رَضِيَ ٱللَّهُ عَنۡهُ who ascribes the words to the Prophet Muḥammad صَلَّى ٱللَّهُ عَلَيۡهِ وَسَلَّمَ rather than Jesus.

14 Here the allusion is to the value of this world in and of itself. That is, God does not look at His creation of this world, rather He looks at humans and all that is in His creation; this world is simply the temporary location in which His creatures are tested. And these tests and actions determine one's final place in the hereafter [eds.]. Ibn Abī l-Dunyā, *Dhamm al-dunyā*, 29 (no. 40), from a *ḥadīth* related on the authority of Ibn Yasār who heard it indirectly (*balāghan*) from the Prophet.

15 Abū Nuʿaym, *Ḥilya*, 2:313; Ibn Abī l-Dunyā, *Dhamm al-dunyā*, 31 (no. 45).

[The Prophet] صَلَّى ٱللَّٰهُ عَلَيْهِ وَسَلَّمَ said, "*Competition in worldly increase diverts you* [Q. 102:1]. The son of Adam says, 'My wealth… my wealth…' But do you possess any of your wealth save what you ate and consumed? Or what you wore and frayed? Or what you gave in charity and thus accomplished [something with]?"[16]

And he صَلَّى ٱللَّٰهُ عَلَيْهِ وَسَلَّمَ said,

> "This world is the abode of [whoever] has no abode. It is wealth for [whoever] has no wealth. Only [one] devoid of intellect amasses it. Only [one] devoid of knowledge feuds over it. Only [one] devoid of understanding envies on account of it. Only [one] devoid of certitude strives for it."[17] | 17

[The Prophet] صَلَّى ٱللَّٰهُ عَلَيْهِ وَسَلَّمَ said,

> Whoever begins [the day] and his greatest worry is this world has nothing to do with God, God will attach four traits to his heart: a worry that he will never relinquish, a preoccupation that he will never free himself from, a poverty that leaves him always in want, and a hope whose end he will never attain.[18]

Abū Hurayra said,

> The Messenger of God صَلَّى ٱللَّٰهُ عَلَيْهِ وَسَلَّمَ said to me, "O Abū Hurayra, shall I show you all of this world and what is in it?"
>
> I replied, "Of course, Messenger of God." He took me by the hand to one of the valleys of Medina, and there [we found] a dunghill containing human skulls, excrement, rags, and bones.

16 Muslim, *Ṣaḥīḥ*, 4:2273 (no. 2958).

17 Cf. Ibn Abī l-Dunyā, *Dhamm al-dunyā*, 92 (no. 182); Ibn Ḥanbal, *Musnad*, 40:480 (no. 24419). Both sources relate a *ḥadīth* on the authority of ʿĀʾisha, رَضِيَ ٱللَّٰهُ عَنْهَا who heard the Prophet صَلَّى ٱللَّٰهُ عَلَيْهِ وَسَلَّمَ say, "This world is the abode of the person who has no abode. It is wealth for the person who has no wealth. Only the person devoid of intellect amasses it." The middle sentence of the *ḥadīth* is included in only one manuscript of Ibn Ḥanbal's *Musnad*, while other manuscripts consulted by the editor omit it.

18 Al-Daylamī, *Musnad al-firdaws*, 3:580 (no. 5818), related on the authority of Ibn ʿUmar رَضِيَ ٱللَّٰهُ عَنْهُمَا. Cf. Ibn Abī l-Dunyā, *Dhamm al-dunyā*, 27 (no. 35), which reads, "Shuʿayb b. Ṣāliḥ said, 'Jesus, son of Mary, عَلَيْهِ ٱلسَّلَامُ said, "This world does not inhabit the heart of a servant except that his heart clings to three things from it…"' The text then omits the first trait.

Then he said, "Abū Hurayra, these skulls used to have aspirations like yours and hopes like your hopes, and now they are skinless bones soon to become ash. This excrement is the color of their food that they acquired from wherever they acquired it. Then they expelled it from their stomachs to become what it is, and people avoid it. These tattered rags were their garments and apparel, and they have become what they are, and the winds flap them about. These bones are the bones of their animals for which they sought pasture from the farthest lands. So whoever would weep over this world, let him weep."

[Abū Hurayra] said, "We did not depart until our own weeping had become intense."[19] | 18

It is related that when God عَزَّوَجَلَّ cast Adam down to earth, He said to him, "Build [knowing that it will be] in ruins; procreate [knowing that the offspring will] perish."[20]

Dāwūd b. Hilāl said,

It is written in the scriptures of Abraham عَلَيْهِ السَّلَامُ, "Oh world! How insignificant are you [this world] to the righteous—for whom you have beautified and ornamented yourself! I have thrust into their hearts hatred and aversion toward you [this world]. I have not created a creation more insignificant than you [this world]. Your entire affair is paltry, and you proceed toward annihilation. The day that I created you [this world], I decreed that you will never endure for anyone and that no one will endure for you, even if your adherent were stingy with you and greedy for you. Blessed are the righteous who have shown Me contentment in their hearts and veracity and steadfastness in their consciences. Blessed are they! What reward do I have in store for them! When they come to me from their graves, light will proceed before them, and the angels will encompass them, until I convey to them what they hoped for of My mercy."[21]

---

19 Al-Ishbīlī, *al-ʿĀqiba*, 50. Al-Zabīdī notes that Abū Ṭālib al-Makkī records it in his *Qūt al-qulūb* on the authority of Ḥasan. Al-Zabīdī, *Itḥāf*, 8:84.

20 Ibn al-Mubārak, *Zuhd*, 111 (no. 258); Abū Nuʿaym, *Ḥilya*, 3:286, reported on the authority of Mujāhid or someone else (*aw ghayrihi*).

21 Abū Nuʿaym, *Ḥilya*, 10:158; Ibn Abī l-Dunyā, *Dhamm al-dunyā*, 63 (no. 115).

The Messenger of God صَلَّى ٱللَّهُ عَلَيْهِ وَسَلَّمَ said,

> This world is suspended between heaven and earth; since its creation God تَعَالَىٰ has not looked at it. It [this world] will say on the day of resurrection, "Oh Lord! Give me the fate of the lowest of your saints on this day." [God] will reply, "Silence, you nothing! I did not desire you [this world] for them [the saints] in their [earthly] lives (*fī l-dunyā*)—should I desire you for them on this day?"[22] | 19

It is related in the reports of Adam عَلَيْهِ ٱلسَّلَامُ that when he ate from the tree his stomach turned so that its dregs would vacate. Nothing like this had been created in the foods of heaven except in this tree, and so he was forbidden to eat from it.

[The narrator] said,

> [Adam] took to wandering around heaven, so God تَعَالَىٰ ordered an angel to address him. [God] told [the angel],
>
> Say to [Adam], "What do you need?"
>
> Adam replied, "I need to rid my stomach of this harm."
>
> Then, it was said to the angel, "Say to him, "Where will you rid yourself of it? On your bedding? Or on your cushions? Or in the rivers? Or under the shade of the trees? Do you think any of these are appropriate places for that? Rather, descend to this world.""[23]

[The Prophet] صَلَّى ٱللَّهُ عَلَيْهِ وَسَلَّمَ said,

> "Groups of people will be brought forth on the day of resurrection, their [good] deeds like the mountains of Tihama. Then it will be ordered that they be [cast] into the fire."

---

22 Abū Ṭālib al-Makkī, *Qūt al-qulūb*, 1:244. Cf. Abū Nuʿaym, *Ḥilya*, 1:72, on the authority of ʿAlī b. Abī Ṭālib رَضِيَ ٱللَّهُ عَنْهُ. A similar *ḥadīth* was reported on the authority of Abū Hurayra رَضِيَ ٱللَّهُ عَنْهُ, who said, "This world is suspended between heaven and earth like an old water skin, crying out to its Lord from the time He created it until the day He annihilates it, 'Oh Lord! Oh Lord! Why do you hate me?' He will then reply to it, 'Silence, you nothing! Silence, you nothing!'" Ibn Abī l-Dunyā, *Dhamm al-dunyā*, 153 (no. 360).

23 Abū Ṭālib al-Makkī, *Qūt al-qulūb*, 1:254.

[The Companions] asked, "Messenger of God, are they [people who] pray?"

He said, "Yes. They would pray and fast and take but little [rest] in the night, but when anything of this world was presented to them, they would pounce on it."[24]

[The Prophet] صَلَّى ٱللَّهُ عَلَيْهِ وَسَلَّمَ said in one of his sermons,

20 The believer is between two terrors: | between a past, about which he knows not what God will do, and a future, for which he knows not what God will decree. So let the servant take provisions [for the journey] from himself for his soul (*nafsihi*),[25] from his worldly [affairs] (*dunyāhu*) for his hereafter, from his life for his death, and from his youth for his old age. For this world was created for you, and you were created for the hereafter. By Him in whose hand is my soul! After death there is no more soliciting of favors [from God], and after this world there is no abode except heaven or the fire.[26]

Jesus عَلَيْهِ ٱلسَّلَامُ said, "Love of this world and [love of] the hereafter cannot stand together in the heart of a believer, just as water and fire cannot stand together in a single receptacle."[27]

It is related that Gabriel عَلَيْهِ ٱلسَّلَامُ said to Noah عَلَيْهِ ٱلسَّلَامُ, "Oh oldest of the prophets! How have you found this world?" He replied, "Like a house with two doors: I entered through one, and I exited through the other."[28]

---

24 Ibn al-Aʿrābī, *al-Muʿjam*, 893 (no. 1865); al-Daylamī, *Musnad al-firdaws*, 5:498 (no. 8875), both on the authority of Anas رَضِيَ ٱللَّهُ عَنْهُ. Cf. Abū Nuʿaym, *Ḥilya*, 1:178, where a similar *ḥadīth* is reported on the authority of Sālim رَضِيَ ٱللَّهُ عَنْهُ.

25 Note that *nafs* can mean "soul" or "oneself," so this could read "from himself for himself" [eds.].

26 Ibn Abī l-Dunyā, *Qiṣar al-amal*, 129 (no. 190), on the authority of Ḥasan; al-Bayhaqī, *Shuʿab al-īmān*, 13:153 (no. 10097), on the authority of Ḥasan who heard it from an unnamed Companion; al-Daylamī, *Musnad al-firdaws*, 3:93 (no. 4261), on the authority of Jābir رَضِيَ ٱللَّهُ عَنْهُ.

27 Ibn Abī l-Dunyā, *Dhamm al-dunyā*, 44–45 (no. 76); al-Dīnawarī, *al-Majālisa wa-jawāhir al-ʿilm*, 200 (no. 1150).

28 Ibn Abī l-Dunyā, *Dhamm al-dunyā*, 110–111 (no. 229); Ibn ʿAsākir, *Tārīkh madīnat Dimashq*, 62:281.

It was said to Jesus عَلَيْهِ ٱلسَّلَامُ, "If you took a house, it would [provide you with] shelter." He replied, "Sufficient for us are the threadbare [garments] of those who came before us."[29] | 21

Our Prophet صَلَّىٱللَّهُعَلَيْهِوَسَلَّمَ said, "Be wary of this world, as it is more bewitching than Hārūt and Mārūt."[30]

Ḥasan [al-Baṣrī], said, "The Messenger of God صَلَّىٱللَّهُعَلَيْهِوَسَلَّمَ approached his Companions one day and said,

> Would any of you want God to remove his blindness and give him sight? Whoever covets this world and holds high expectations of it, God will certainly blind his heart to the same degree. Whoever denies himself in this world and holds low expectations of it, God will give him knowledge without studying and righteous guidance without direction from another.[31] After you there will come a people for whom this worldly dominion will only be established [lit., stand] with killing and brute force (*tajabbur*), and affluence [will] only [be gained] with pride and avarice, and love [will] only [be given] by following desires. Whoever reaches that time and endures poverty, though he is capable of affluence, and endures hatred, though he is capable of love, and endures baseness, though he is capable of high standing—and does all this wanting nothing more than the countenance of God تَعَالَىٰ—God عَزَّوَجَلَّ will give him the reward of fifty of His veracious ones (*ṣiddīq*).[32]

It was related that one day Jesus عَلَيْهِ ٱلسَّلَامُ faced extreme rain, thunder, and lightning, so he began looking for something in which to take shelter. A tent was pitched for him a ways away. He went to it and found a woman inside, so he left her. He then found a mountain cave and went to it only to find a lion inside. He placed his hand on [the lion] | and said, "My God, you have made a refuge for everything, but you have not made one for me." God تَعَالَىٰ then revealed (*awḥā*) 22

29 Ibn Abī l-Dunyā, *Dhamm al-dunyā*, 69 (no. 129).

30 Ibn Abī l-Dunyā, *Dhamm al-dunyā*, 69–70 (no. 132); al-Bayhaqī, *Shuʿab al-īmān*, 13:103–104 (no. 10022), on the authority of Abū l-Dardāʾ al-Ruhāwī. Hārūt and Mārūt are two angels of Babylon mentioned in Q. 2:102.

31 *Hudan bi-ghayri hidāya.*

32 Ibn Abī l-Dunyā, *Kitāb al-zuhd*, 62 (no. 105); al-Bayhaqī, *Shuʿab al-īmān*, 13:153–154 (no. 10098); Abū Nuʿaym, *Ḥilya*, 6:312.

to him, "Your refuge is a permanent place in My mercy." On the day of resurrection, I will marry you to one hundred *ḥūrī*s who I created with My own hand. And I will feed [those attending] your wedding feast for four thousand years, each day of which is like the duration of this world. And I will order a herald to call out, Where are the ascetics (*zuhhād*) of this world? Come to the wedding feast of the ascetic Jesus son of Mary!"[33]

Jesus son of Mary عَلَيْهِ ٱلسَّلَامُ, said,

> Woe to the adherent of this world (*ṣāḥib al-dunyā*)![34] How he will die and leave it and all that it contains. [How] he is faithful to it, yet it deceives him. [How] he trusts it, yet it forsakes him. Woe to the deluded ones! How [this world] has shown them what they despise. [How] what they love has left them, and what they have been promised has come to them. Woe to he whose worry is for this world and whose actions are misdeeds! How he will be disgraced tomorrow for his sin.[35]

It has been said, "God عَزَّوَجَلَّ revealed to Moses عَلَيْهِ ٱلسَّلَامُ,

> Oh Moses! What business do you have with the oppressors' abode? It is not an abode for you. Leave your worry and separate [yourself] from it using your mind, for it is the worst of abodes, except for one who does [righteous] deeds in it, for then it is the best of abodes. Oh Moses! I watch the oppressor until I take from him [what is due for the] oppressed.[36]

It was related that the Messenger of God صَلَّى ٱللَّهُ عَلَيْهِ وَسَلَّمَ dispatched Abū ʿUbayda b. al-Jarrāḥ [to the frontier], and he returned with

---

33 Ibn Abī l-Dunyā, *Kitāb al-zuhd*, 64 (no. 111); Ibn ʿAsākir, *Tārīkh madīnat Dimashq*, 47:421, on the authority of Muḥammad b. Sibāʿ al-Numayrī.

34 Note that the phrase *ṣāḥib al-dunyā*, translated here and throughout as "adherent of the world," could also indicate someone who possesses (i.e., a possessor of) something of this world, or someone who cares more about or is fully engrossed in this world and heedless of the hereafter.

35 Ibn Abī l-Dunyā, *Dhamm al-dunyā*, 52–53 (no. 92), on the authority of ʿUbaydallāh b. Muslim.

36 Ibn Abī l-Dunyā, *Dhamm al-dunyā*, 53 (no. 93), on the authority of ʿUbāda Abū Marwān.

wealth from Bahrain.[37] The Anṣār heard news of Abū ʿUbayda's return, and they prayed *fajr* | with the Messenger of God ﷺ. When the Messenger of God ﷺ finished praying, he went to leave, so they intercepted him. The Messenger of God ﷺ smiled when he saw them and said, "I suspect that you have heard that Abū ʿUbayda returned with something?" They said, "Yes, indeed, oh Messenger of God." He replied, "Then rejoice and have hope in what will make you happy, for—by God—I do not fear poverty for you. Rather, I fear for you that this world will be granted to you just like it was to those before you, and you will compete over it just like they did, and it will destroy you just as it destroyed them."[38]

23

Abū Saʿīd al-Khudrī said,

> The Messenger of God ﷺ said, "What I fear most for you is what God brings forth for you from the blessings[39] of the earth."
>
> It was then asked, "What are the blessings of the earth?"
>
> He replied, "The splendor of this world."[40]

The Messenger of God ﷺ said, "Do not busy your hearts with the remembrance of this world."[41] Thus he forbade the remembrance of it, much less attaining [the world] itself.

ʿAmmār b. Saʿīd said,

> Jesus عَلَيْهِ ٱلسَّلَام passed by a village and [found] its residents dead in the courtyards and streets. He said, "Oh you assembly of disciples! These [people] surely died in a state of | anger, for had they died otherwise, they would have buried one another."

24

37 As explained in the full version of the *ḥadīth* found in Muslim (*Ṣaḥīḥ*, 4:2273–2274 [no. 2961]), the wealth was the *jizya* paid by the people of Bahrain.

38 Al-Bukhārī, *Ṣaḥīḥ*, 4:96–97 (no. 3158); Muslim, *Ṣaḥīḥ*, 4:2273–2274 (no. 2961).

39 Here the Prophet is expressing his fear that although these blessings are good in themselves they may preoccupy Muslims with this world to the detriment of their work for the hereafter [eds.].

40 Muslim, *Ṣaḥīḥ*, 2:728 (no. 1052); cf. al-Bukhārī, *Ṣaḥīḥ*, 4:26–27 (no. 2842). See Q. 20:131, which refers to *zahrata al-ḥāyati al-dunyā*, that is, "the splendor of the life of this world," which has been given to some of the disbelievers to enjoy.

41 Ibn Abī l-Dunyā, *Dhamm al-dunyā*, 122 (no. 264); al-Bayhaqī, *Shuʿab al-īmān*, 13:155 (no. 10100), on the authority of Muḥammad b. al-Naḍr al-Ḥārithī. Al-Zabīdī, *Ithāf*, 8:87.

[The disciples] said, "Oh spirit of God [i.e., Jesus] we wish to know their story."

So [Jesus] asked his Lord, and God تَعَالَىٰ revealed to him, "When it is nighttime, call on them [the dead], and they will answer you." When nighttime came, he looked down from an elevated plane and called out, "Oh people of this village!"

A villager came back, "At your service, spirit of God!"

[Jesus] asked, "What is your condition, and what is your story?"

They said, "We entered the night [safe and] sound (*fī ʿāfiyya*) and awoke in an abyss."[42]

[Jesus] said, "How is that so?"

[A respondent] said, "Because of our love of this world and our obedience to the people of sin."

[Jesus] asked, "How was your love of this world?"

[The villager] said, "Like the love of a child for its mother: when she gave him attention we rejoiced, and when she turned away we grieved and wept."

[Jesus] asked, "What about your companions who did not answer me?"

He said, "[They answer not] because they are restrained with reins of fire that are in the hands of angels, harsh and severe."[43]

[Jesus] asked, "Then how is it that you, among [all of] them, answer me?"

He replied, "Because I was among them, but I was not like them. When [God's] torment descended on them, it struck me along with them. So I am suspended on the precipice of hell, I do not know if I will be delivered from it or cast into it."

The Messiah then said to his disciples, "Eating barley bread with coarse salt, wearing coarse wool, and sleeping on discarded [cloth]—this is a lot, with well-being [in] this world and in the hereafter."[44]

Anas said,

> The Messenger of God صَلَّى ٱللَّٰهُ عَلَيْهِ وَسَلَّمَ had a camel named al-ʿAḍbāʾ who could not be outrun. A Bedouin came with a

---

42 Cf. Q. 101:9: *His refuge will be an abyss.*

43 See Q. 66:6 for the same description of the angels of hell.

44 Ibn Abī l-Dunyā, *Dhamm al-dunyā*, 128–129 (no. 282); Ibn Abī l-Dunyā, *Kitāb al-zuhd*, 132–133 (no. 298).

> young camel and beat her in a race, and the Muslims were troubled by this. So the Messenger of God صَلَّى ٱللَّٰهُ عَلَيْهِ وَسَلَّمَ said, "It is appropriate for God to never elevate anything of this world without humbling it."[45] | 25

Jesus عَلَيْهِ ٱلسَّلَامُ said, "Who is the one who would build a home on the waves of the sea? Such is this world for you, so do not take it as a [permanent] abode."[46]

It was said to Jesus عَلَيْهِ ٱلسَّلَامُ, "Teach us one deed that God will love us for doing." He said, "Detest this world. God تَعَالَىٰ will love you."[47]

Abū l-Dardāʾ said,

> The Messenger of God صَلَّى ٱللَّٰهُ عَلَيْهِ وَسَلَّمَ said, "If you knew what I know, you would seldom laugh, and you would weep a great deal. This world would seem insignificant to you, and you would favor the hereafter."

Then Abū l-Dardāʾ himself said,

> If you knew what I know, you would go off into the desert, supplicating and weeping for your souls. You would leave your wealth unguarded, never returning to it save for what is absolutely necessary of it.[48] But [in fact] remembrance of the hereafter is absent from your hearts, while hope [of this world] has occupied them. So this world has become more suited to your deeds,[49] and you have become like those who do not know.[50] Some of you are worse than the beasts who do not desist from their passions in fear of their consequences.

---

45 Al-Bukhārī, *Ṣaḥīḥ*, 4:32 (no. 2872). Al-Zabīdī writes, "There exists in the penmanship of al-Kamāl al-Damīrī [d. 808/1405] the words, 'One of the students of knowledge informed me that he heard a memorizer of the Qurʾān saying, "The Bedouin who came on a young camel and beat the camel of the Prophet صَلَّى ٱللَّٰهُ عَلَيْهِ وَسَلَّمَ was Gabriel عَلَيْهِ ٱلسَّلَامُ."'" Al-Zabīdī, *Itḥāf*, 8:88.

46 Ibn Abī l-Dunyā, *Dhamm al-dunyā*, 156 (no. 370), on the authority of Saʿīd b. ʿAbd al-ʿAzīz; Ibn ʿAsākir, *Tārīkh madīnat Dimashq*, 47:430, on the authority of Mujāhid.

47 Ibn Abī l-Dunyā, *Dhamm al-dunyā*, 170 (no. 415), on the authority of Salam b. Bashīr.

48 I.e., the minimal amount needed to sustain life [eds.]..

49 *Amlaka bi-aʿmālikum*. See Lane, *An Arabic-English Lexicon*, 7:2730 (s.v. م - ل - أ).

50 See Q. 39:9: *Say, Are those who know equal to those who do not know?*

What is [the matter] with you that you do not love one another nor counsel one another though you are brothers in God's *dīn*? What has divided you into sects is nothing but the malice of your hearts. If you were to unite in righteousness, you would love one another. | 26

What is [the matter] with you that you counsel one another in regard to this world but not in regard to the hereafter? None of you has advice for the one he loves and [none of you] assists him in regard to his hereafter. This is only because of the lack of faith in your hearts. If you were certain of the good and the evil of the hereafter in the manner that you are certain of this world, you would prefer to seek the hereafter, as it is more suited to your affairs.

Were you to say, "Love of what is immediate[ly at hand] predominates," [we would reply] that we advise you to leave what is immediate in this world for the future [in the hereafter]. You exhaust yourselves in hardship and [mastering] a profession while seeking something that you might not attain. You are the worst of people. You have not realized your faith according to what is known among you as the "utmost faith."[51] If you have misgivings about what Muḥammad ﷺ brought, come to us, and let us explain clearly to you and show you the light that will fill your hearts with tranquility. By God! You are not intellectually stunted so that we might excuse you. You demonstrate the correct opinion in your worldly affairs (*dunyākum*), and you exercise prudence in this regard.

What is [the matter] with you that you rejoice when you attain but a little of this world and you grieve when just a little of it slips away from you? [You do this] until it becomes evident on your faces and manifests on your tongues, as you call [the loss of something] "misfortunes, and you [practically] perform funeral rites for them. The common people among you have left behind much of their *dīn*, and yet [concern over] this is not

51 *Al-īmān al-bāligh*, that is, faith that reaches the utmost point or degree, which appears to be a play on words in reference to Q. 68:39: *Or do you have oaths [binding] upon Us, extending until the day of resurrection…*

evident on your faces, while no one's condition changes because of you. Truly, I see that God has absolved [Himself] of you.

You meet one another happily, while every one of you hates to receive his friend in an offensive manner, fearing that his friend might receive him in a similar manner. So you have taken one another as companions out of spitefulness.[52] Your pastures have sprouted | in dung; you have built mutual affection by denying your appointed death (*ajal*). I wish that God تَعَالَىٰ would relieve me of you and unite me with the one I long to see [again]![53] Were he alive, he would not tolerate you. If there is any good in you, then I have told you [in detail]. If you seek what is with God, you will find it with ease. And I seek God's aid for myself and for you.[54]

27

Jesus عَلَيْهِ ٱلسَّلَامُ said, "Oh you disciples! Content yourselves with what is inferior of this world but with soundness in your *dīn*, just as worldly people (*ahl al-dunyā*) content themselves with what is inferior in their *dīn* but with soundness in this world."[55]

It has been said [in poetic verse] to the same effect:

I see men who are satisfied with the most inferior [practice] of *dīn*,
Though I do not see them content with shortfalls in life.
So through *dīn* be free of need of the worldly possessions (*dunyā*) of kings,
Just as these kings, through their worldly possessions, have no need of *dīn*.[56]

52 Read *fa-ṣṭaḥabtum* for *fa-aṣbaḥtum*, in accordance with the wording that appears in al-Zabīdī, *Itḥāf*, 8:89.

53 In light of the next sentence Abū l-Dardāʾ is clearly talking about the Prophet.

54 Ibn Abī l-Dunyā, *Dhamm al-dunyā*, 173–174 (no. 427). For the initial words of the Prophet, see al-Bukhārī, *Ṣaḥīḥ*, 6:54 (no. 4621); Muslim, *Ṣaḥīḥ*, 4:1832 (no. 2359), on the authority of Anas رَضِيَ ٱللَّهُ عَنْهُ.

55 Ibn Abī l-Dunyā, *Dhamm al-dunyā*, 179 (no. 449), on the authority of Zakariyyā b. ʿAdī.

56 The origins of these two couplets are disputed. See Ibn al-Mubārak, *Dīwān al-Imām*, 117–118 (no. 57); Ibn Qutayba al-Dīnawarī, *ʿUyūn al-akhbār*, 2:372 (attributed to Abū l-ʿAtāhiyya); al-Warrāq, *Dīwān*, 281 (no. 227); and Ibn Manẓūr, *Mukhtaṣar Tārīkh Dimashq*, 4:32 (attributed to Ibrāhīm b. Adham). The meter of

Jesus عَلَيْهِ ٱلسَّلَامُ said, "Oh seeker of this world, give in charity! Your
28 abandonment of this world is more righteous."[57] |

Our Prophet صَلَّىٱللَّهُعَلَيْهِوَسَلَّمَ said, "After me there is sure to come to you worldly [riches] that will consume your faith like fire consumes wood."[58]

God تَعَالَىٰ revealed to Moses عَلَيْهِ ٱلسَّلَامُ, "Oh Moses! Do not fall back on love of this world, for you will not come before Me with a major [sin] worse for you than this."[59]

Moses عَلَيْهِ ٱلسَّلَامُ passed a man who was weeping, and he returned and [still the man] was weeping. So Moses said, "Oh Lord! Your servant is weeping out of fear of you." [God] replied, "Oh son of ʿImrān! Were his brains to fall along with the tears of his eyes, and were his hands to rise up [to me in supplication] until they fell off, I would not forgive him as long as he loves this world."[60]

The Traditions (*āthār*)

ʿAlī رَضِيَ ٱللَّهُ عَنْهُ said, "Whoever brings together six traits will not pass up any desire for heaven nor any escape from the fire: He is the one who recognizes God and then obeys Him; [who] recognizes Satan and defies him; [who] recognizes the truth and follows it; [who] recognizes falsehood and then protects [himself] from it; [who] recognizes this world and rejects it; [and who] recognizes
29 the hereafter and seeks it."[61] |

---

the poem is *basīṭ*. For a concise treatment of the fifteen meters of Arabic poetry, see Stoetzer, "Prosody (*ʿarūḍ*)," 619–622.

57 Al-Zabīdī writes, "Its meaning is, Oh you who seek this world to be righteous by giving it away! (Thus, he is not seeking it for its own sake.) Your abandoning it is more righteous than giving it away in charity." Al-Zabīdī, *Itḥāf*, 8:90.

58 Al-Zabīdī, *Itḥāf*, 8:90. In his *ḥadīth* collection al-Marwazī relates on the authority of Abū Thaʿlaba al-Khushanī رَضِيَ ٱللَّهُ عَنْهُ, "Rejoice in a vast world that will consume your faith." See al-Marwazī, *Kitāb al-Fitan*, 39 (no. 121).

59 Cf. Abū Nuʿaym, *Ḥilya*, 6:5.

60 Al-Zabīdī cites Ibn Abī l-Dunyā's *Dhamm al-dunyā*. Al-Zabidī, *Itḥāf*, 8:90.

61 Al-Zabīdī cites Ibn Abī l-Dunyā's *Dhamm al-dunyā*. Al-Zabīdī *Itḥāf*, 8:90.

Ḥasan [al-Baṣrī] said, "God has mercy on those people who treated this world like a trust that they returned to the one who entrusted them with it, and so they departed unencumbered."[62]

[Ḥasan al-Baṣrī] رَحِمَهُ ٱللَّهُ also said, "Whoever competes with you in your *dīn*, compete with him. Whoever competes with you in this world, throw it down before him."[63]

Luqmān عَلَيْهِ ٱلسَّلَامُ said to his son,

> My son, this world is a deep sea in which many people have drowned. So let your ship that is on it be the fear of God عَزَّوَجَلَّ, while its cargo is faith in God عَزَّوَجَلَّ, and its sail is trust in God عَزَّوَجَلَّ. Perhaps then you will be saved, though I do not think that you are saved.[64]

Al-Fuḍayl [b. ʿIyāḍ] said, "Long have I reflected on this verse: *Indeed, We have made that which is on the earth adornment for it that We may test them* [*as to*] *which of them is best in deed. And indeed, We will make that which is upon it* [*into*] *a barren ground* [Q. 18:7–8]."

A wise man said,

> You will come upon nothing of this world except what was possessed by people before you and what will be possessed by people after you. There is nothing for you from this world except dinner at night and lunch in the day, so do not fall into ruin over a meal. Fast from this world, and break your fast with the hereafter. This world's capital is desire, and its profit is the fire.[65] | 30

62 According to al-Zabīdī, Abū Ṭālib al-Makkī transmitted this tradition in *Qūt al-qulūb*. Al-Zabīdī, *Itḥāf*, 8:90.

63 According to al-Zabīdī, Abū Ṭālib al-Makkī transmitted this tradition in his *Qūt al-qulūb*. Al-Zabīdī, *Itḥāf*, 8:91. Ibn Abī Shayba relates a similar tradition from Ḥasan, "Whenever you see a man competing in this world, compete with him over the hereafter." Ibn Abī Shayba, *al-Muṣannaf*, 19:369 (no. 36351).

64 Ibn al-Mubārak, *Zuhd*, 184 (no. 537).

65 Al-Zabidī cites Ibn Abī l-Dunyā's *Dhamm al-dunyā* as a source for this text. al-Zabīdī, *Itḥāf*, 8:91.

It was asked of a monk,

"How do you regard fate (*dahr*)?"[66]

He said, "It creates the bodies, renews hopes, draws death nearer, and drives away the object of desire."

It was said, "What of [God's] people?"

He [the monk] said, "Whoever is victorious over it[67] tires, and whoever loses it [this world] is drained."[68]

And about this, it was said,

Whoever praises this world because of a delight in life,

By my life! He will rebuke it before long.

When [this world] slips away, it is source of grief for a person,

And if it draws near, profuse are its worries.[69]

A wise man said,

This world existed, and I was not in it. This world will go, and I will not be in it. So I do not feel at home in it. For life in it is hardship, its purity is muddied, and its people are in constant fear of it, either [of] a vanishing blessing, or an oncoming affliction, or a decreed death.[70]

One of [the wise men] said, "One of the flaws of this world is that it does not give a person what he deserves. Rather, it gives him more [than what he deserves], or [it gives] him less."[71]

---

66 "Fate" is a translation of *dahr*, which Lane translates as (possibly) a name of God, "the Efficient of fortune," because the Prophet equates it with God in some ḥadīths. Lane, *An Arabic-English Lexicon*, 3:923 (s.v. د - ه - ر). See Muslim, *Ṣaḥīḥ*, 4:1762 (no. 2246).

67 "It" here and in the remainder of the sentence could refer to "this world" or "fate" [eds.].

68 For the first part of this tradition, see al-Kharāʾiṭī, *Iʿtilāl al-qulūb*, 1:47 (no. 90). The editor of the Dār al-Minhāj edition of the *Iḥyāʾ* notes that some manuscripts have the alternative *naṣiba* in place of the last word (translated above) *naḍaba*. The former carries a similar meaning of "to become fatigued" or "wear himself out."

69 ʿAlī b. Abī Ṭālib, *Dīwān*, 354 (no. 374). The meter of the poem is *ṭawīl*.

70 Cf. Abū Nuʿaym, *Ḥilya*, 2:136, where the second part of this tradition appears in a letter that Ḥasan wrote to ʿUmar b. ʿAbd al-ʿAzīz.

71 The statement is attributed to Bozorgmehr. Al-Ābī, *Nathr al-durr*, 7:67 (no. 73).

Sufyān [b. ʿUyayna] said, "Would you not say that blessings are like a curse?[72] They are granted to the undeserving (*fī ghayri ahlihā*)."[73] | 31

Abū Sulaymān al-Dārānī said,

> Whoever seeks this world out of love for it will be given something and [then] desire more, and whoever seeks the hereafter out of love for it will be given something and [then] desire more.[74] And for this there is no end, and for that there is no end.[75]

A man said to Abū Ḥāzim,

> "I complain to you of my love for this world, though it is not my [true] abode."
>
> He replied, "Look. Whatever God عَزَّوَجَلَّ offers you from it, take only of it what is lawful, and put it only toward what is due to Him, and love for this world will do you no harm."[76]
>
> [Abū Ḥāzim] merely said this because if [the man] were to blame himself for this, it would tire him until he became fed up with this world and might seek to leave it.

Yaḥyā b. Muʿādh said, "This world is Satan's shop, so do not steal anything from his shop, lest he come to reclaim it and take you!"[77]

Al-Fuḍayl [b. ʿIyāḍ] said, "If this world were made of gold that perishes and the hereafter were made of clay that endures, it would be incumbent on us to choose clay that endures over gold that perishes. So how is it that we chose clay that perishes over gold that endures?"[78]

Abū Ḥāzim said, "Beware of this world! I was informed that on the day of resurrection the servant | who used to revere this world 32

---

72 *Maghḍūbun ʿalayhā*, that is, an object of [God's] anger. Cf. Q. 1:7.

73 Al-Khaṭīb al-Baghdādī, *Tārīkh Baghdād*, 10:375.

74 Lit., whoever seeks this world out of love for it will be given nothing of it except that he desires more, and whoever seeks the hereafter out of love for it will be given nothing of it except that he desires more [eds.].

75 Al-Zabīdī cites Abū Nuʿaym's *Ḥilya* as a source for this text. Al-Zabīdī, *Itḥāf*, 8:91.

76 Al-Bayhaqī, *Shuʿab al-īmān*, 9:503 (no. 7021).

77 Al-Zabīdī cites Ibn Abī l-Dunyā's *Dhamm al-dunyā* as a source for this text. Al-Zabīdī, *Itḥāf*, 8:92.

78 Al-Zabīdī cites Abū Nuʿaym's *Ḥilya* as a source for this text. Al-Zabīdī, *Itḥāf*, 8:92.

will be detained, and it will be said, 'This [one] revered what God debased.'"[79]

Ibn Masʿūd said, "No person begins the day except as a guest, and his wealth is borrowed; [when] the guest departs, the loan is returned."[80]

And [about this] it has been said,

> What are wealth and family but a trust,
> And one day all trusts must be returned.[81]

Rābiʿa's companions visited her and started speaking of this world, so they engaged in censure of [the world]. She said, "Stop mentioning it, for if there were not a place for it in your hearts, you would not mention it so much. Surely, whoever loves something mentions it constantly."[82]

It was said to Ibrāhīm b. Adham, "How are you?" He replied,

> We patch this world by tearing up our *dīn*,
> So neither our *dīn* nor what we patch remains.
> Blessed then is a servant who preferred God as his Lord,
> And sacrificed this world for what he hopes for.[83] | 33

And it has been said,

> I see the seeker of this world—though his life is long
> Attain happiness and blessings from this world
> Like a builder who builds his edifice and raises it up,
> And when it is level, what he has built collapses.[84]

---

79 Al-Zabīdī cites Ibn Abī l-Dunyā's *Dhamm al-dunyā* and Abū Nuʿaym's *Ḥilya* as sources for this text. Al-Zabīdī, *Itḥāf*, 8:92.

80 Al-Ṭabarānī, *al-Muʿjam al-kabīr*, 9:105 (no. 8533); Abū Nuʿaym, *Ḥilya*, 1:134.

81 Al-ʿĀmirī, *Dīwān*, 89. The meter of the poem is *ṭawīl*.

82 Ibn Abī l-Dunyā, *Dhamm al-dunyā*, 184 (no. 464).

83 The first verse is attributed to both ʿAdī b. Zayd al-ʿIbādī and ʿAbdallāh Ibn al-Mubārak. See al-ʿIbādī, *Dīwān*, 200 (no. 156); Ibn al-Mubārak, *Dīwān al-Imām*, 148 (no. 21). For a discussion of the two verses together, see Ibn ʿAbd al-Barr, *Bahjat al-majālis*, 3:289, n. 2. The meter of the poem is *ṭawīl*.

84 Ibn Abī l-Ḥadīd, *Sharḥ Nahj al-balāgha*, 19:291. The meter of the poem is *ṭawīl*.

It was said,

> Flee this world and it will come to you spontaneously.
> Is not transferral its destiny?
> And what is your world but a shadow:
> It shaded you and then foreshadowed its departure.[85]

Luqmān said to his son, "My son, sell your world for your hereafter and you will gain both; do not sell your hereafter for your world or you will lose them both."[86]

Muṭarrif b. ʿAbdallāh b. al-Shikhkhīr said, "Do not look to the easy life of kings and their luxurious attire. Rather, look to the speed with which they depart and their violent overthrow."[87]

Ibn ʿAbbās said, "God تَعَالَىٰ has made this world into three parts: a part for the believer, a part for the hypocrite, and a part for the disbeliever. The believer provisions himself [for the hereafter], the hypocrite adorns [himself], and the disbeliever enjoys himself."[88] | 34

One of them said, "This world is a corpse, so whoever desires something from it, let him endure the company of dogs."[89]

About this it was said:

> Oh you who ask this world for her hand in marriage!
> Abandon courting her and you will be safe
> The one whom you court is treacherous;
> The wedding is closer to a funeral.[90]

---

85 Ibn Abī l-Ḥadīd, *Sharḥ Nahj al-balāgha*, 19:291. Cf. Abū l-ʿAtāhiyya, *Abū l-ʿAtāhiyya*, 297 (and see n. 9). The meter of the poem is *wāfir*.

86 Ibn Abī l-Dunyā, *Dhamm al-dunyā*, see al-Zabīdī, *Itḥāf*, 8:92. Cf. Abū Nuʿaym, *Ḥilya*, 2:143, where the speaker is not Luqmān but Ḥasan.

87 Al-Dīnawarī, *al-Majālisa wa-jawāhir al-ʿilm*, 394 (no. 2299).

88 Al-Zabīdī cites Ibn Abī l-Dunyā's *Dhamm al-dunyā* as a source for this text. Al-Zabīdī, *Itḥāf*, 8:93.

89 Cf. Abū Nuʿaym, *Ḥilya*, 8:238, where a similar tradition is reported from ʿAlī (may God ennoble his face).

90 The two verses are attributed to Abū l-ʿAtāhiyya, *Abū l-ʿAtāhiyya*, 644 (no. 246). The meter of the poem is *sarīʿ*.

Abū l-Dardāʾ said, "what [makes] this world despicable to God is that He is only disobeyed in it and His reward is only attained by abandoning it."[91]

And [about this] it has been said,

> When an intelligent person examines this world, it reveals itself
> To him as an enemy in the clothing of a friend.[92]

It was also said,

> Oh you who sleep the night happy with its onset!
> Calamities may indeed strike just before daybreak.
> Destroying the ages that were full of comfort,
> The back-and-forth, incessant return of day and night
> How many a king did the vicissitudes of fate destroy?
> Who, in his time, was a [great] source of benefit and harm?
> Oh you who embrace a world that does not remain!
> Who ends and begins [each day] in this world a [perpetual] traveler! |
> Why not forsake embracing this world,
> so that you can embrace virgins in al-Firdaws?
> If you desire to dwell in the gardens of eternity,
> Do not feel safe from the fire.[93]

35

Abū Umāma al-Bāhilī رَضِيَ اللَّهُ عَنْهُ said,

"When Muḥammad صَلَّى اللَّهُ عَلَيْهِ وَسَلَّمَ was sent [to humanity], Satan's troops came to him and said, 'A prophet has been sent and a new community has emerged.'[94]

[Satan] said, 'Do they love this world?'

They replied, 'Yes.'

He said, 'If they are wont to love it, it does not concern me if they do not worship idols. I will go back and forth to

91 See al-Dīnawarī, *al-Majālisa wa-jawāhir al-ʿilm*, 309 (no. 1805), where the statement is attributed to an unnamed wise man.

92 The verse is attributed to Abū Nuwās, *Dīwān*, 714. The meter of the poem is *ṭawīl*.

93 The verses are attributed to [Muḥammad b. Ḥāzim] al-Bāhilī, *Dīwān al-Bāhilī*, 56. The meter of the poem is *ṭawīl*.

94 Cf. Q. 3:110: *You are the best community ever raised for humanity…*

them [with] three [temptations]: taking money without right, squandering it without right, and withholding it from [whom it is] due. And all evil follows from these.'"[95]

A man once said to ʿAlī رَضِيَ ٱللَّهُ عَنْهُ,

"Oh commander of the faithful! Describe this world to us."

He replied, "What I describe to you is an abode in which whoever is healthy never feels secure, whoever is sick regrets, whoever is poor [feels] sorrow, and whoever is rich is tested. There is reckoning [on the day of judgment] for what is lawful, punishment for what is unlawful, and reprimand for what is ambiguous."[96]

The same was said to him another time, and he replied, "The long [version] or the short?" It was said, "[The] short [version]." So [ʿAlī] said, "[what is] lawful [will be] accounted [for], and [what is] unlawful [will be] punished."[97]

Mālik b. Dīnār said, "Be wary of the sorceress, for she bewitches the hearts of scholars."[98] That is, this world. | 36

Abū Sulaymān al-Dārānī said,

Whenever the hereafter is in the heart, this world comes to crowd it. But whenever this world is in the heart, the hereafter does not crowd it, as the hereafter is generous and this world is stingy.[99] This is especially harsh, and we hope that what Sayyār b. al-Ḥakam related is more accurate; he said, "This world and the hereafter gather in the heart, so whichever one dominates, the [heart] will follow it."[100]

Mālik b. Dīnār said, "Worry over the hereafter leaves your heart to the degree that you grieve over this world; worry over this world

95 Ibn Abī l-Dunyā, *Dhamm al-dunyā*, 17 (no. 10).

96 Cf. Ibn Abī l-Dunyā, *Dhamm al-dunyā*, 21 (no. 18), which reads, "...an abode in which whoever is healthy feels secure."

97 Ibn Abī l-Dunyā, *Dhamm al-dunyā*, 20 (no. 17).

98 Here sorceress and the pronoun are feminine because the *dunyā* (this world) is feminine in Arabic [eds.]. Ibn Abī l-Dunyā, *Dhamm al-dunyā*, 29 (no. 39).

99 Ibn Abī l-Dunyā, *Dhamm al-dunyā*, 66 (no. 121).

100 Ibn Abī l-Dunyā, *Dhamm al-dunyā*, 65–66 (no. 120). Al-Zabīdī says that this name should be Sayyār Abū l-Ḥakam; see al-Zabīdī, *Itḥāf*, 8:94.

leaves your heart to the degree that you grieve over the hereafter."[101] This is an adaptation of what ʿAlī [b. Abī Ṭālib] (may God ennoble his face) said "This world and the hereafter are [like] two wives, to the extent that one of them is pleased, the other is displeased."[102]

Ḥasan said, "By God! I have encountered people to whom this world was as insignificant as the dirt they walk on. They do not care about this world, if the sun rises or sets, if it [this world] goes this way, or if it goes that way."[103]

A man once said to Ḥasan,

> "What do you say about a man to whom God gave wealth, and he gives [some of] it in charity and brings [people] together, and does right with it? Is it right for him to subsist on it?" Meaning, live a life of ease with it?
>
> 37 He replied, "No. | Were he to possess this world in its entirety, none of it would be for him except for sustenance, and he sets that aside for the day that he is in need."[104]

Al-Fuḍayl said, "If this world in its totality were presented to me lawfully, I would not be accountable for it in the hereafter, I would avoid it [in disgust] like one of you avoids the carcass that sullies your clothes when you pass by it."[105]

It was said,

> ʿUmar رَضِيَ ٱللَّهُ عَنْهُ arrived in Shām [greater Syria], and Abū ʿUbayda b. al-Jarrāḥ received him on the back of a camel tied with rope halter. [ʿUmar] greeted him and asked about him. Then [ʿUmar] came to his home and saw nothing inside but his sword, his shield, and his saddle. ʿUmar رَضِيَ ٱللَّهُ عَنْهُ said to him, "If you would only take some furnishings."

---

101 Ibn Abī l-Dunyā, *Dhamm al-dunyā*, 66 (no. 122).

102 Ibn Abī l-Dunyā, *Dhamm al-dunyā*, 65 (no. 119), where the statement is attributed to Wahb b. Munabbih.

103 Abū Nuʿaym, *Ḥilya*, 6:272.

104 Abū Nuʿaym, *Ḥilya*, 6:198.

105 Abū Nuʿaym, *Ḥilya*, 8:89.

He replied, "Oh commander of the faithful! This [my worldly goods] will allow us to reach the [true] resting place."[106]

Sufyān [al-Thawrī] said, "Take from this world [what suffices] for your body, and take from the hereafter for your heart."[107]

Ḥasan [al-Baṣrī] said, "By God! The children of Israel worshiped idols after worshiping the All-Merciful because of their love of this world."[108]

Wahb [b. Munabbih] said,

> I read in a book, this world is gains (*ghanīma*)[109] for the clever and heedlessness for the ignorant [who] did not realize [the nature of the world] until they were departing from it; they asked to return, but they [could] not return.[110] | 38

Luqmān said to his son, "Oh my son! You turned away from this world from the day you came into it and turned toward the hereafter. [Now] you are closer to an abode you are advancing to and farther than from an abode you are distancing yourself from."[111]

Saᶜd b. Masᶜūd said, "When you see a servant who, when his worldly possessions increase and his hereafter dwindles, he is pleased. That is the one who is deceived, who fidgets with his face unaware."[112]

ᶜAmr b. al-ᶜĀṣ said from the *minbar*, "By God! I have never seen a people more covetous of what the Messenger of God صَلَّىٱللَّهُعَلَيْهِوَسَلَّمَ denied himself than you. By God! Not three [people] passed by the Messenger of God صَلَّىٱللَّهُعَلَيْهِوَسَلَّمَ except that [he] owes more than what he possessed."[113]

Ḥasan [al-Baṣrī] said, after reciting His تَعَالَىٰ words, *So let not the worldly life delude you and be not deceived about God by the deceiver*

106 Ibn al-Mubārak, *Zuhd*, 197 (no. 586). "[True] resting place" (*al-maqīl*) is a reference to heaven, in light of Q. 25:24: *The companions of paradise, that day, are* [*in*] *a better settlement and better resting place.*

107 Abū Nuᶜaym, *Ḥilya*, 7:20.

108 Abū Nuᶜaym, *Ḥilya*, 6:198.

109 Here the translation is "gains" because *ghanīma*, which is usually translated as spoils, loot, or booty, are considered negative and/or illegal in English and here it is not meant in that sense [eds.].

110 Ibn Abī l-Dunyā, *Dhamm al-dunyā*, 40 (no. 65).

111 Ibn Abī l-Dunyā, *Dhamm al-dunyā*, 43 (no. 73).

112 Ibn Abī l-Dunyā, *Dhamm al-dunyā*, 54 (no. 96).

113 Ibn Abī l-Dunyā, *Dhamm al-dunyā*, 58–59 (no. 106).

[Q. 35:5], "Who said this? Who created it and who knows best? Beware of the distractions of this world, for many are the distractions of this world. A man does not open a door of distractions for himself except that this door opens ten more for him."[114]

[Ḥasan al-Baṣrī] also said,

> The poor son of Adam. He is content with an abode, the lawful [of which] he is accountable for, and the unlawful [of which] are a punishment. If he takes from [what] is lawful, he is accountable for His blessing, and if he takes from [what] is unlawful, he is punished | for it. The son of Adam considers his wealth meager, but does not consider his [good] deeds meager. He rejoices at his misfortune in his *dīn*, and he is anguished by his misfortune in his worldly [state].[115]

39

Ḥasan [al-Baṣrī] wrote to ʿUmar b. ʿAbd al-ʿAzīz (God's mercy be on them both) "Peace be on you. To proceed: It is as though you are with the last [person] for whom death has been written, [and] he has died." ʿUmar replied, "Peace be on you. It is as though you were never in this world, and you never ceased to be in the hereafter."[116]

Al-Fuḍayl b. ʿIyāḍ said, "Entering into this world is easy, but freeing oneself from it is onerous."[117]

Some of them said,

> How strange is the one who knows that death is real, how [can he be] joyous? How strange is the one who knows that the fire is real, how can he laugh? How strange is the one who sees this world turning upside down on its people, how can he be at ease with it? How strange is the one who knows that predestination is real, how can he exhaust [himself]?[118]

---

114 Ibn Abī l-Dunyā, *Dhamm al-dunyā*, 60–61 (no. 110).

115 Ibn Abī l-Dunyā, *Dhamm al-dunyā*, 103–104 (no. 211).

116 Ibn Abī l-Dunyā, *Qiṣar al-amal*, 146–147 (no. 226); cf. Abū Nuʿaym, *Ḥilya*, 5:305.

117 Ibn Abī l-Dunyā, *Kitāb al-zuhd*, 164 (no. 397).

118 Ibn Abī l-Dunyā, *Dhamm al-dunyā*, 109–110 (no. 227), where the passage is part of a longer report by Misʿar b. Kidām.

A man from Najran who was two hundred years old came to Muʿāwiya رضي الله عنه, and [Muʿāwiya] asked him about this world and how he experienced it.

> [The man] replied, "[I have had] some years of affliction, and some years of abundance. Day after day and night after night, a baby is born and a person perishes. Were it not for the newborns, people would become extinct. Were it not for the deceased, this world would be overcrowded."
>
> [Muʿāwiya] then said to him, "Ask for what you wish."
>
> He said, | "[I wish for] life that has passed, that you bring it back, or delay an appointed [death]." 40
>
> [Muʿāwiya] said, "I am not capable of this."
>
> [The man] said, "There is nothing I need from you."[119]

Dāwūd al-Ṭāʾī رحمه الله said, "Oh son of Adam! You rejoiced when you achieved your hope, and yet you attained it with the end of your appointed [term]. Then you put off [doing] your [good] deeds, as if the benefit were for someone other than you."[120]

Bishr b. al-Ḥārith [al-Ḥāfī] said, "Whoever asks God for this world, he is merely asking Him to prolong [his time] standing before Him."[121]

Abū Ḥāzim [Salma b. Dīnār al-ʿAraj] said, "There is nothing that makes you happy in this world except that it comes with something that will harm you."[122]

Ḥasan [al-Baṣrī] said, "The soul of the son of Adam does not depart from this world except with three regrets: he was not satisfied with what he amassed, he did attain what he hoped for, and he did not adequately provision [himself] for his destination [the hereafter]."[123]

---

119 Ibn Abī l-Dunyā, *Dhamm al-dunyā*, 113–114 (no. 239).

120 Ibn Abī l-Dunyā, *Dhamm al-dunyā*, 115 (no. 243).

121 Lit., "between His hands," meaning that his questioning on the day of judgment will be prolonged and this is a form of punishment [eds.]. Ibn Abī l-Dunyā, *Dhamm al-dunyā*, 120 (no. 261).

122 Ibn Abī l-Dunyā, *Dhamm al-dunyā*, 121–122 (no. 263).

123 Ibn Abī l-Dunyā, *Dhamm al-dunyā*, 126 (no. 275).

It was once said to a worshiper, "You have attained affluence." He said, "Only the one who has been freed from slavery to this world 41 has attained affluence."[124] |

Abū Sulaymān [al-Dārānī] said, "[One] cannot be patient [to resist] the temptations of this world unless he is [fully] engaged with [working toward] the hereafter."[125]

Mālik b. Dīnār said, "We have made peace [among ourselves] with the love of this world, and thus we do not command one another [to good] nor forbid one another [from evil]. God did not call us to do this. Woe to me, which of God's punishments will befall us!"[126]

Abū Ḥāzim said, "A little [gain in] this world distracts from much [of the work for] the hereafter."[127]

Ḥasan [al-Baṣrī] said, "Despise this world, for by God, the one who has it is not happier than the one who despises it."[128]

He also said, "When God wants good for a servant, He gives him a bit of this world and then holds back. When it runs out, He restores it to him. If a servant is of no importance to Him, He grants this world to him liberally."[129]

One of them used to supplicate, "Oh You who holds the heavens back from falling to the earth save by your permission! Hold [abundance in] this world back from me!"[130]

Muḥammad b. al-Munkadir said,

> Have you not considered that if a man were to fast without break [lit., for eternity], 42 | and stand [in prayer all] night without letting up, and give his wealth in charity, and strive in the path of God, and abstain from what God made unlawful; still he will be brought forward on the day of resurrection, and [God] will say, "Here is the one! Verily what was great in his eyes

124 Ibn Abī l-Dunyā, *Dhamm al-dunyā*, 126 (no. 276).

125 Ibn Abī l-Dunyā, *Dhamm al-dunyā*, 129 (no. 284). The report was transmitted from Abū Sulaymān indirectly (*balāghan*).

126 Ibn Abī l-Dunyā, *Dhamm al-dunyā*, 133 (no. 297).

127 Ibn Abī l-Dunyā, *Dhamm al-dunyā*, 134–135 (no. 305).

128 Ibn Abī l-Dunyā, *Dhamm al-dunyā*, 138–139 (no. 314). Al-Zabīdī records a different wording of this tradition in which Ḥasan says, "Despise this world, for by God, you will be happier when you despise it." Al-Zabīdī, *Itḥāf*, 8:96.

129 Ibn Abī l-Dunyā, *Dhamm al-dunyā*, 139 (no. 315).

130 Ibn Abī l-Dunyā, *Dhamm al-dunyā*, 139 (no. 317).

was little to God, and [what was] little in his eyes was great to God!" How do you think he will fare? Who among us is not like this? The world is [considered] great to us, even while we commit sins and misdeeds.[131]

Abū Ḥāzim said,

Provisions for this world and for the hereafter have become hard [to attain]. As for provisions for the hereafter, you will find no one to support you in them. As for provisions for this world, you hardly reach your hand toward a thing before you find that some reprobate has beaten you to it.[132]

Abū Hurayra said,

This world is suspended between heaven and earth like an old water skin crying out to its Lord from the time He created it until the day He annihilates it, "Oh Lord! Oh Lord! Why do you hate me?"

So, [God] replies to it, "Silence, oh you [who are] nothing! Silence, oh you [who are] nothing!"[133]

ʿAbdallāh b. al-Mubārak said, "Love of this world is in the heart and sins have surrounded it, so when will any good reach it?"[134]

Wahb b. Munabbih said, "The one whose heart rejoices in anything of this world has failed to attain wisdom. Whoever puts his desire beneath his feet, Satan fears his shadow. | And the one whose knowledge prevails over his passion is the one who triumphs."[135] 43

It was said to Bishr, "So-and-so has died."

He replied, "He amassed [wealth in] this world and went on to the hereafter, he has lost his soul!"

It was said to him that [the person] would do this and would do that, and they recounted various sorts of righteous behavior.

131 Ibn Abī l-Dunyā, *Dhamm al-dunyā*, 140–141 (no. 321).
132 Ibn Abī l-Dunyā, *Dhamm al-dunyā*, 142 (no. 325).
133 Ibn Abī l-Dunyā, *Dhamm al-dunyā*, 153 (no. 360).
134 Ibn Abī l-Dunyā, *Dhamm al-dunyā*, 177 (no. 437).
135 Ibn Abī l-Dunyā, *Dhamm al-dunyā*, 180 (no. 452).

> He replied, "What benefit [to him] is this when he amassed [wealth in] this world?"[136]

One of them [an ascetic] said, "This world makes itself loathesome to us, and yet we love it. Then what if were to endear itself to us?"[137]

It was said to a wise man, "To whom does this world belong?" He said, "To the one who abandons it." Then it was said, "To whom does the hereafter belong?" He said, "To the one who seeks it."[138]

A wise man said, "This world is the abode of ruin, and what is more ruined than it is the heart of one who cultivates it [this world]. Heaven is the abode of prosperity, and what is more prosperous than it is the heart of one who seeks it."[139]

Al-Junayd said,

> Al-Shāfiʿī رَحِمَهُ ٱللَّٰهُ was one of those who desire God and who speak with the voice of truth in this world. He admonished one of his brothers in God and filled him with the fear of God.
>
> Then [al-Shāfiʿī] said, "Brother, this world is indeed a slippery place and an abode of humiliation. Prosperity in it becomes ruin, and its inhabitants repair to the graves. Its integrity rests on estrangement, and its riches lead to poverty. Abundance in it | is impoverishment, and impoverishment in it is affluence. So flee to God, and be content with God's sustenance. Do not borrow from your permanent abode [the hereafter] for your ephemeral abode [this world], for your life is a vanishing shadow and a leaning wall. Increase your good deeds and decrease your hope [for this world]."

44

Ibrāhīm b. Adham said to a man, "Is a dirham in your dreams more desirable to you or a dinar while awake?"[140]

> He replied, "A dinar while awake."

136 Ibn Abī l-Dunyā, *Dhamm al-dunyā*, 183 (no. 459).
137 Ibn Abī l-Dunyā, *Dhamm al-dunyā*, 185 (no. 470).
138 Ibn Abī l-Dunyā, *Dhamm al-dunyā*, 187 (no. 476).
139 Ibn Abī l-Dunyā, *Dhamm al-dunyā*, 187 (no. 477).
140 A dirham was a silver coin; a dinar was a gold coin [eds.].

> [Ibrāhīm] said, "You have misspoken, because what you love in this world is what you love in your dreams, while what you do not love in the hereafter is what you do not love while awake."[141]

On the authority of Ismāʿīl b. ʿAyyāsh who said, "Our companions would call this world a pig, saying, 'Get away from us, pig!' If they had found a name for it more vile than this, they would have called it that."[142]

Kaʿb said, "This world will endear itself to you until you worship it and its people."[143]

Yaḥyā b. Muʿādh al-Rāzī رَحِمَهُ ٱللَّٰهُ said, "The intelligent [ones] are three: one who abandons this world before it abandons him; one who prepares his grave before entering it; and one who pleases his Creator before meeting Him."[144]

He also said, "The accursedness of this world has reached the point that your desire for it distracts you from obedience to God. So how can [anyone] become ensnared in it?"

Bakr b. ʿAbdallāh said, "Whoever wants to be free of this world while in this world | is like the one who extinguishes fire with straw."[145] 45

Bandār said, "When you see the children of this world speaking about asceticism, know that they are Satan's laughingstock."[146]

He also said, "Whoever turns toward this world, its fires—that is, avarice—will incinerate him until he becomes ash. Whoever turns toward the hereafter, its fires will purify him, and he will become an ingot of gold that benefits [all]. And whoever turns toward God عَزَّوَجَلَّ, the fires of God's oneness will incinerate him, and he will become a priceless jewel."

---

141 Ibn Abī l-Ḥadīd, *Sharḥ Nahj al-balāgha*, 19:292. The world is like a silver coin in a dream, the hereafter is like a gold coin while awake [eds.].

142 Cf. Ibn Abī l-Dunyā, *Dhamm al-dunyā*, 147 (no. 347), in which Ismāʿīl reports a similarly worded tradition on the authority of Abū Rāshid al-Tanūkhī who heard it from Yazīd b. Maysara.

143 Ibn Abī l-Dunyā, *Kitāb al-zuhd*, 73 (no. 140).

144 Al-Bayhaqī, *Kitāb al-zuhd al-kabīr*, 198 (no. 488).

145 Al-Dīnawarī, *al-Majālisa wa-jawāhir al-ʿilm*, 92 (no. 548).

146 Al-Zabīdī explains, "That is, only an ascetic should speak about self-denial so that his words have effect." Al-Zabīdī, *Itḥāf*, 8:98.

ʿAlī رَضِيَ اللَّهُ عَنْهُ said,

> This world is but six things: [what is] eaten, drunk, worn, ridden, married, and scented. So the noblest of foods is honey, while this is the watery milk of an insect. The noblest of drinks is water, while both the righteous and the reprobate have equal [access to it]. The noblest of clothing is silk, while this is the [spun] thread of worms. The noblest of mounts is the horse, while men are slain on it. The noblest of mates is the woman, while [this relation involves] a urethral opening into another. By God! A woman adorns the most beautiful thing in herself, while the most unpleasant [part] of her is desired. And the noblest of scents is musk, and it is the blood of an animal.[147]

147 Cf. al-Rāghib al-Iṣfahānī, *al-Dharīʿa*, 218.

2

An Elucidation of the Exhortations on the Censure of This World and [Explaining] Its Nature

46

SOMEONE said, Oh people! Work slowly, and fear God عَزَّوَجَلَّ. Do not let expectation and forgetfulness of your appointed death deceive you. Do not rely on this world, for it is a treacherous imposter. It has adorned itself for you with its deceptions, seduced you with its [objects of] desire, and adorned itself for its suitors. Thus it has become like the unveiled bride: all eyes gaze on her, all hearts are obsessed by her, and all souls long for her. But how many a lover has she killed, and how many a tranquil [person] has she forsaken?

Look to [this world] with the eye of truth, for it is an abode with abundant misfortunes, and its Creator condemned it. Its newness decays, while dominion over it fades away. The [one who is] mighty in it is despised, while its abundance decreases. The living dies, and its good passes away. So wake up from your heedlessness—may God have mercy on you—and arise from your sleep, before it is said, "So-and-so is ill, or is weighed down by [debilitating] disease." Is there [anyone] to point to the [right] medicine? Is there any way [to reach] the physician? So the physicians are called for you, but no cure is expected. Then it will be said, "So-and-so has made his will and tallied his wealth." Then it will be said, "His tongue has grown heavy, so he cannot speak to his brothers, and he does not recognize his neighbors." At that point your brow has begun to sweat, and your moans ensue. Your certainty [of dying] is fixed, your eyes [lit., eyelids] have turned toward [death], and your doubts [that you might die] have proven true. Your tongue stammers, and your brothers weep. It is said to you, "This is your son so-and-so; this is your brother so-and-so." You have been deprived of speech, so you do not utter [a word]. Your tongue has been sealed, and it cannot be freed. Then the decree befalls you. Your soul has been plucked from your limbs and then is raised to the heavens. | At that point your brothers have gathered, and your death shrouds have been brought. They have washed you and shrouded you. Then your visitors withdraw, and those envious of you are relieved. Your family has left to be with your wealth, while you remain captive to your deeds.

47

Someone said to one of the kings,

> The person most justified in censuring and detesting this world is the one who was given abundance in it and whose need of it has been met because [this person] expects some peril to assail his wealth and sweep it away, or [take] what he has accumulated and scatter it, or uproot his authority from its foundations,[1] or creep into his body and sicken him, or afflict him by stripping him of something beloved that he hoards. Thus, this world is more deserving of censure: it takes what it gives, it takes back what it grants. In making its master laugh, it makes others laugh at him. In weeping for him, it makes others cry for him. In extending its palm in giving, it extends it to reclaim [it]. Today it places the crown on the head of its master, and tomorrow it covers him in dirt. What perishes and what lives on are the same to it; it finds in the living a successor for what perishes, and it is content with the replacement of everything.[2]

Ḥasan al-Baṣrī wrote to ʿUmar b. ʿAbd al-ʿAzīz,

> To proceed: This world is an abode of departure, not an abode of residency. Adam عَلَيْهِ السَّلَامُ was sent down to it from the garden as a punishment. Be wary of it, oh commander of the faithful. [Taking] provisions from it is abandoning it, and affluence from it is impoverishment. In every moment [someone] dies. It debases whoever cherishes it, and it impoverishes whoever

1 Cf. Q. 16:26: ... *But God came at* [i.e., uprooted] *their building from the foundations...*

2 Ibn Abī l-Dunyā, *Kitāb al-zuhd*, 39 (no. 47).

accumulates [wealth]. It is like the poison ingested by one who is oblivious, which [is] his demise. Be in it like one treating his wound: abstain | for a short time out of fear of what he detests in the long run, and endure the severity of the medicine out of fear of a protracted affliction. 48

Be wary of this treacherous, duplicitous, deceiving abode that has adorned itself with its deceptions, seduced with its delusions, beautified itself with its hopes, and longed for (*tashawwaqat*)[3] its suitors. Thus it has become like the unveiled bride: [all] eyes gaze on her, hearts are in rapture over her, and souls long for her, and yet she is the death of every one of her spouses. The living takes no heed of the deceased, the last [person] is not rebuked by the [experience of the] first, and the gnostic of God عَزَّوَجَلَّ, once apprised of its [nature], remembers not. Her lover no sooner obtains his need of her than he is deluded, and [becomes] a tyrant, and forgets the return [to God]. He busied his mind with her until he lost his footing. His regret then became immense, and his grief multiplied. The pangs of death conspired against him with pain, and the sorrows of missed [opportunities were] agony for him. [A person] desirous of her never obtains from her what he seeks and never finds rest for himself from his toil. Thus he set out without [any] provisions, never to reach a resting place. Beware of her, oh commander of the faithful.

You will be happier in [this world], the more wary you are of it. For, whenever the master of this world feels secure enough in it to be happy, it dispatches him to [something] detestable. Happiness in it for its people is deception, and benefit from it is harm tomorrow. Prosperity from it comes with affliction, while permanence in it brings about annihilation. Thus happiness in it is adulterated with sorrows. What is close slips away and does not return, and we do not know what is coming to anticipate [it].

[All] hopes for it are lies, and expectations of it are falsehoods. Its purest portion is muddied, and life in it is hardship. The

3 Alternatively, al-Zabīdī has *tashawwafat* (spruced itself up). Al-Zabīdī, *Itḥāf*, 8:100.

son of Adam is in danger in it. Were he to use his intellect and reflect, he would [recognize] the gravity of [worldly] abundance and would be wary of danger. Even if the Creator had not informed [humanity] about it and set forth a parable for it, | [the danger of] this world would still have awoken the sleeper and roused the heedless. How much more so then when an admonition about it has come from God عَزَّوَجَلَّ and an exhorter has appeared in it?[4] So [this world] has no value before God—lofty be His praise—and He has not paid attention to it since its creation.[5]

49

It was presented to your Prophet صَلَّى ٱللَّهُ عَلَيْهِ وَسَلَّمَ with all its keys and its treasures, [and were he to have accepted it], this would not diminish God's [kingdom] by the equivalent of a gnat's wing. But he refused to accept it,[6] as he loathed violating God's command, or loving what his Creator detests, or exalting what his Master abases. [God] then concealed [this world] from the righteous to test [them], and He gave amply of it [the wealth of this world] to His enemies to delude [them].

The one deluded by it, who has mastery over it, thinks that honor has been bestowed on him. He has forgotten what God عَزَّوَجَلَّ did to Muḥammad صَلَّى ٱللَّهُ عَلَيْهِ وَسَلَّمَ when he tied a stone over his belly.[7] An account has come from him on the authority of his Lord تَبَارَكَ وَتَعَالَىٰ that He said to Moses عَلَيْهِ ٱلسَّلَامُ, 'When you see affluence coming your way, say, "[It is] a sin whose punishment has been deferred." When you see poverty coming your way, say, "Welcome to the badge of the righteous!"'[8] And if you wished, you might take as your example the one entrusted with

4 The former is a reference to the Qurʾān, and the latter is a reference to the Prophet.

5 For context, see p. 8, n. 14 [eds.].

6 Al-Tirmidhī relates a *ḥadīth* on the authority of Abū Umāma in which the Prophet صَلَّى ٱللَّهُ عَلَيْهِ وَسَلَّمَ said, "My Lord offered to turn the valley of Mecca into gold for me. I said, 'No, oh Lord. I would rather satisfy my appetite one day and go hungry the next.'" Al-Tirmidhī, *Sunan*, 4:575 (no. 2347).

7 For the full context of the twenty-seven-day siege that took place during the Battle of the Trench, see al-Bukhārī, *Ṣaḥīḥ*, 5:108 (no. 4101). The Prophet used to tie a stone to his belly to stop the pangs of hunger [eds.].

8 The tradition is related by al-Daylamī from Abū Saʿīd رَضِيَ ٱللَّهُ عَنْهُ. Al-Daylamī, *Musnad al-firdaws*, 3:175 (no. 4469).

[God's] spirit and word, Jesus, son of Mary عَلَيْهِ ٱلسَّلَامُ. [Jesus] used to say, 'My seasoning is hunger. My badge is fear [of God]. My clothing is wool. My warmth in the winter is the rising sun. My lantern is the moon. My riding beast is my two legs. My food and my fruits are what the earth sprouts. I sleep and I have nothing, and I wake and I have nothing. And there is no one on earth richer than I.'"[9] | 50

Wahb b. Munabbih said, "When God عَزَّوَجَلَّ sent Moses and Aaron عَلَيْهِمَا ٱلسَّلَامُ to Pharaoh, [God] said, 'Do not let his attire, which is the attire of this world, frighten you. His forelock is in My hand: he does not speak, blink, or breathe except with My permission. Do not let what he enjoys of [worldly pleasures] astonish you, for they are [merely] the splendors of the life of this world and the adornment of those [living] in ease.[10] Had I wished to adorn you in this world—Pharaoh would realize, when he sees it, that he is impotent in comparison to what you have been given—I would have done so. But I disliked that for you, and so I kept [this world] away from you like I do with My saints: I drive them away from its comforts, just like the compassionate herdsman drives his sheep away from dangerous pastures. I [God] turn [My saints] away from its diversions, just like the compassionate herdsman turns his camels away from resting places [that are full] of mange. This is not because they are insignificant to Me, but [it is] so that they might attain their full share of My favor, in abundance and without deficit. My saints only beautify themselves for me with meekness, awe, fear, and humility. Piety is firmly established in their hearts and so appears on their bodies. Thus, it is their garment that they wear, their covering that they display, their conscience that they sense, their salvation that they achieve, their hope that they harbor, their grandeur on which they pride themselves, and their mark by which they are recognized. Then, if you

9 Ibn Abī l-Dunyā, *Kitāb al-zuhd*, 40–43 (no. 50); Abū Nuʿaym, *Ḥilya*, 6:313–314, both on the authority of Ḥasan.

10 See Q. 20:131: *And do not extend your eyes toward that by which We have given enjoyment to* [*some*] *categories of them,* [*its being but*] *the splendor of worldly life by which We test them.*

were to meet them, be gentle toward them,[11] and humble your heart and your tongue before them. And know that whoever threatens | My saint has entered into war with Me, and I will be [the saint's] avenger on the day of resurrection.'"[12]

51

ʿAlī رَضِيَ اللَّهُ عَنْهُ was giving a sermon one day and said,

Know that you will die and will be resurrected after death; you will be informed of your deeds and recompensed for them. Therefore, do not let the life of this world deceive you, for it is surrounded by affliction, infamous for annihilation, and defined by treachery. Everything in it is vanishing, and among its people it takes turns and alternates.[13] Its states do not persist, and its denizens are never safe from its evil. As soon as its people [find] prosperity and happiness in it, they are in affliction and deceived, [they are in] alternating states and vicissitudes; life in it is blameworthy, and prosperity in it never persists. Its people are mere targets while in it: it pelts them with its arrows and shatters them with death. Every person's demise in it is decreed and his share in it is complete.

Servants of God, know that you and whatever [state] you are in this world you are on the path of those who have passed before—[the path of] those who lived longer than you, [who were] mightier than you, [who were] more prolific in construction than you, and [whose] vestiges reached farther than yours. After all of the ups and downs, their voices then fell still and silent, their bodies decayed, their homes were left empty and in ruins, and their traces were effaced.

They exchanged lofty palaces and comfortable beds and pillows for stones and rocks that rest on hollowed-out graves that are split [into the ground]. Their location [in the graves] is close, while their residents are exiles among the desolate people of

11 Lit., "lower your wing to them." Cf. Q. 15:88: ... *And lower your wing to the believers.*

12 Ibn Abī l-Dunyā, *Kitāb al-zuhd*, 46–47 (no. 62); Abū Nuʿaym, *Ḥilya*, 1:11–12.

13 *Sijālun*, literally "buckets," when applied in the context of war, means alternating portions of victory, like two people who alternate in dropping their buckets into a well to attain their respective portions. Lane, *An Arabic-English Lexicon*, 4:1311 (s.v. س - ج - ل).

dwellings and [among] the preoccupied people of settlements. They take no notice of the civilization [above them], and they do not associate with one another in the manner of neighbors and siblings, notwithstanding | their closeness, their dwelling next to one another, and the proximity of their home. How can there be any association between them when decay has ground them down heavily, and the stones and soil have consumed them? They have become dead after having lived, and after a life of plenty [they have become] crumbling bones.

52

Their loved ones were pained [by their deaths], while they dwelled under the dirt. They departed with no [way to] return—how preposterous would that be [to expect a return]! *No! It is only a word he is saying; and behind them is a barrier until the day they are resurrected* [Q. 23:100]. So, it is as though you have already arrived at their same state of decay and isolation in your final resting place. You have been received in that bed as a pledge; that depository has enclosed you.

So how would you be if you were to survey the state of affairs when the graves are scattered, *and that* [*what is*] *within the breasts is obtained* [*uncovered*] [Q. 100:10], and you are called to account before the Majestic King. So hearts would fly away out of fear of their past sins, all veils and coverings would be torn from you, and your defects and secrets would appear. It is there that every soul will be recompensed for what it earned. Verily God عَزَّوَجَلَّ says, *That He may recompense those who do evil with* [*the penalty of*] *what they have done and recompense those who do good with the best* [*reward*] [Q. 53:31]. And He تَعَالَىٰ said, *The record* [*of deeds*] *will be placed* [*open*], *and you will see the criminals fearful of that within it, and they will say, "Oh, woe to us! What is this book that leaves nothing small or great except that it has enumerated it?" And they will find what they did present* [*before them*]. *And your Lord does injustice to no one* [Q. 18:49]. May God make all of us act in accordance with His book and follow His saints so that—out of His favor—He might settle us all in the abode of continuance. And He is praised and beneficent."[14]

One of the wise men said,

The days are arrows, and the people are targets. Fate strikes 53 you | with its arrows every day and destroys you, night by night and day by day, until it claims every part of you. So how much remains of your health with the days setting in on you and the speed of the nights [are felt] in your body? If it were revealed to you what damage the days were causing in you, you would have an aversion to every day that comes to you, and you would find the hours passing you by troublesome. But the design of God سُبْحَانَهُ is beyond consideration. It is by forgetting the calamities of this world that enjoyment of its pleasures can be found, while [this world] is more bitter than the colocynth when the physician tests it.[15] Through [this world's] outward acts, it has rendered [the one who] describes its defects sick, while the wonders that it offers are more than what the admonisher can fully encompass. And so we ask God to guide [us] to what is right.[16]

One of the wise men said, after being asked to describe this world and the extent of its duration,

This world is but a blink of your eye. For whatever has passed you by, its attainment has eluded you, and what has not come you have no knowledge of. Fate is a day that is advancing, its own night laments it, and its hour conceals it. Its events continually unfold on people [in the form of] change and loss. Fate is charged with breaking up groups, unsettling unified

14 Ibn Abī l-Dunyā, *Kitāb al-zuhd*, 98–100 (no. 212); al-Dīnawarī, *al-Majālisa wa-jawāhir al-ʿilm*, 364 (no. 2130).

15 The word used here, *ʿajm*, (i.e., tested) alludes to the preparation of medicine by a physican or chemist. In al-Ghazālī's time, medication was often bitter and/or painful. He uses the metaphor of medication throughout his works [eds.].

16 Abū Nuʿaym, *Ḥilya*, 10:150; Ibn Abī l-Dunyā, *Dhamm al-dunyā*, 96–97 (no. 196).

[people], and reshuffling fortunes.[17] Hopes are long, while life is short. And [all] matters go back to God.[18]

ʿUmar b. ʿAbd al-ʿAzīz (may God's mercy be on him) was giving a sermon and said,

Oh people! You | have been created for a matter that, if you believe it, then you are foolish, and if you deny it, then you are ruined. You have been created for eternal [existence], but you will be transferred from abode to abode. Oh servants of God! You are in an abode in [which some of] your food [makes you] choke and your drink is a cause for gasping.[19] A blessing that you find happiness in will not give itself completely to you, unless you leave something else that you are loathe to leave. So, work for [the abode] that you are destined for, in [which you will] remain forever. 54

Then tears overwhelmed him and he descended [from the pulpit].[20]

ʿAlī رَضِيَ ٱللَّهُ عَنْهُ said in [one of] his sermons,

I advise you to fear God and to abandon this world that will abandon you even though you are loathe to abandon it; [this world] that will cause your bodies to decay even though you might desire their rejuvenation. The similitude of you and [this world] is like that of some travelers who set out on a path, and it is as if they have already traversed it. They hastened toward a signpost, and it is as if they have already reached it. How many [a person] will follow the course until he reaches its end? How many [a person] has only a day left in this world, while an eager seeker summons him to leave it? So, do not fret on account of its misfortunes and hardships, for these will come to an end. And do not rejoice in its comforts, for these will fade away. I have been astonished by the seeker of this world

---

17 "Fortunes" here is *duwal* (sing. *dawla*), which implies alternating turns of fortunes on the battlefield or in trade between groups of people. See Lane, *An Arabic-English Lexicon*, 3:934–935 (s.v. د - و - ل).

18 Ibn Abī l-Dunyā, *Dhamm al-dunyā*, 97 (no. 197).

19 Cf. Q. 73:13: *And food that chokes and a painful punishment.*

20 Ibn Abī l-Dunyā, *Dhamm al-dunyā*, 112 (no. 234).

while death seeks him, and by a heedless [person who death] has not forgotten.[21]

Muḥammad b. al-Ḥusayn said,[22]

When the people of intellect, knowledge, gnosis, and etiquette learned that God عَزَّوَجَلَّ despises this world, that He does not wish it on His saints, that it is a despicable and insignificant thing in His estimation, that the Messenger of God صَلَّى ٱللَّهُ عَلَيْهِ وَسَلَّمَ renounced 55 it, and that he warned his Companions | of its temptations, they ate from it in moderation and gave away any excess. They took from it what sufficed and abandoned what distracted [them]. They wore clothing that concealed their nakedness and ate the least amount of food to stave off hunger. They looked at this world with an eye to its ephemerality and at the hereafter with [an eye to] its permanence. Then they took provisions from this world like the mounted traveler [does],[23] thus they ruined their worldly [life][24] and built their hereafter with it. They looked toward the hereafter with their hearts and knew that they would [one day] look at it with their eyes. Thus they set out for it with their hearts when they knew that [one day] they would set out for it with their bodies. They endured patiently for a short time and [will] live in comfort [in the hereafter] for a long time. All of this is through the success [given to them] by their Master, the Generous. They loved what He loved for them, and they detested what He detested for them.

21 Ibn Abī l-Dunyā, *Dhamm al-dunyā*, 169–170 (no. 414).

22 In other manuscripts the name is recorded as Muḥammad b. al-Ḥasan.

23 Al-Zabīdī explains that the mounted traveler (*rākib*) can only pack what is absolutely essential. Al-Zabīdī, *Itḥāf*, 8:105.

24 That is, they did not do anything for their worldly benefit, but worked for the worldly benefit of others; for example, in establishing institutions to benefit and ease the lives of others, so they can concentrate on working for the hereafter [eds.].

3

An Elucidation of the Character of This World Through Examples

56

Know that this world is swiftly fading away, soon to elapse. It promises permanence, then fails to fulfill. You look at it and see it as stationary and stable, while it is furiously marching by and rapidly moving away. Yet [one who] looks at it may not perceive its movement, and so he is tranquil in it. He only perceives [its movement] when it elapses.

[The world's] example is like the shadow, it is in motion and stationary. In reality it is in motion; ostensibly it is stationary. Its motion cannot be grasped with [one's] outward vision but through inward discernment.[1]

When this world was mentioned to Ḥasan al-Baṣrī, رَحِمَهُ ٱللَّهُ he recited [the verse]:

> [Like] dreams from a sleep or like a fading shadow
> The [person] of understanding is not deceived by the likes of it.[2]

1 Cf. al-Ghazālī, *al-Munqidh*, 33.

2 The verse has been attributed to both ʿImrān b. Ḥiṭṭān and Ibn Abī Ḥaṣīna. For the former, see ʿAbbās, *Shiʿr al-Khawārij*, 17 (no. 29). For the latter, see Ibn Abī Ḥaṣīna, *Dīwān*, 1:376. Also see Ibn Abī l-Dunyā, *Kitāb al-zuhd*, 31 (no. 23), where it is attributed to Ḥasan al-Baṣrī. The meter of the poem is *kāmil*.

Ḥasan b. ʿAlī b. Abī Ṭālib رَضِيَ ٱللَّهُ عَنْهُمَا frequently quoted [these words], saying,[3]

> Oh people [seeking] the pleasures of a world that has no permanence!
> It is folly to be deluded by a fading shadow.[4]

57 It has been said [that] this is his own verse. |

It is said that a Bedouin camped with a group. They offered him food, and so he ate. Then he went to the shade of one of their tents and slept there. They [later] pulled up their tent, and so the sun struck him. When he awoke and rose, he said:

> Surely this world is like a shadow that you have cast,
> And one day your shadow will inevitably fade.[5]

Similarly it has been said:

> A man whose biggest worry is this world
> clings to it by a rope of deception.[6]

[Here is] another example

This world, in its capacity to delude with illusions then [leaves] one empty handed once it slips away; it resembles fantasies of sleep and bewildering dreams.

The Messenger of God صَلَّى ٱللَّهُ عَلَيْهِ وَسَلَّمَ said, "This world is a dream, and its people are rewarded and punished [on account of it]."[7]

Yūnus b. ʿUbayd said, "I only liken myself in this world to a sleeping man [who] sees in his sleep what he loathes and what he desires. So when he is like that, he awakens."[8] Similarly, people are | 58

3 My addition of "frequently" (*kathīran*) here is taken from the al-Zabīdī, *Itḥāf*, 8:107 (see base text in margin).

4 Al-Zamakhsharī, *Rabīʿ al-abrār*, 1:70; Ibn al-Jawzī, *al-Mudhish*, 1:395. Ibn Abī l-Dunyā, *Kitāb al-zuhd*, 31 (no. 24). The meter of the poem is *basīṭ*.

5 Ibn Abī l-Dunyā, *Dhamm al-dunyā*, 23 (no. 25); Ibn Abī l-Dunyā, *Kitāb al-zuhd*, 32 (no. 25). The meter of the poem is *ṭawīl*.

6 Al-Zamakhsharī, *Rabīʿ al-abrār*, 1:46. The meter of the poem is *ṭawīl*.

7 Al-Zabīdī, *Itḥāf*, 8:107.

8 Ibn Abī l-Dunyā, *Kitāb al-zuhd*, 31 (no. 21).

sleeping, and when they die, they awaken.[9] Then they have nothing in their possession to rely on and to rejoice in.

A wise man was asked, "What thing most resembles this world?" He replied, "The dreams of the sleeper."[10]

Another example of this world is its enmity toward its people and its destruction of its own children

Know that it is the nature of this world to first lure, slowly and surreptitiously, and [then] to reach destruction in the end. It is like a woman who beautifies [herself] for her suitors until she marries them and slaughters them.

It has been related that this world was unveiled to Jesus عَلَيۡهِ ٱلسَّلَامُ, and he saw it in the form of a fully adorned toothless crone. So he said to her, "How many have you wed?" She replied, "I cannot count them." He said, "Did they all die [with] you, or did they [all] divorce you?" She replied, "[No,] I killed all of them." Jesus عَلَيۡهِ ٱلسَّلَامُ then said, "Wretched be your remaining husbands! How did they not heed your previous husbands? How can you destroy them one after another, and [still] they are not wary of you?"[11] | 59

[Here is] another example of this world and the contradiction of its inner and outward [form]

Know that this world is outwardly adorned and secretly ugly. It resembles a crone who adorns herself, [thereby] deceiving people with her outward [form]. So if they were to become aware of her inner [nature] and lift the veil from her face, her ugliness would be visible to them. Then they would regret pursuing her and be ashamed of their feeble-mindedness in being deceived by her outward [form].

9 This statement has been attributed to both Sufyān al-Thawrī and ʿAlī b. Abī Ṭālib. Al-Zabīdī, *Itḥāf*, 8:107.

10 Ibn Abī l-Dunyā, *Dhamm al-dunyā*, 22 (no. 22).

11 Ibn Abī l-Dunyā, *Dhamm al-dunyā*, 24 (no. 27).

Al-ʿAlāʾ b. Ziyād said,

I saw in my sleep an old crone with wrinkled skin wearing all the adornments of this world. The people were obsessed with her, marveling and gazing at her. I came and looked and was astonished at their gazing at her and their devotion to her, and so I said to her, "Woe to you! Who are you?"

She replied, "Do you not recognize me?"

I said, "No, I do not know who you are."

She said, "I am this world!"

I said, "I seek refuge in God from your evil!"

She said, "If you desire to be protected from my evil, then detest money."[12]

Abū Bakr b. ʿAyyāsh said,

While sleeping I saw this world as a disfigured, white-haired crone. She was clapping her hands, and behind her [numerous] people followed, clapping and dancing. When she was facing me, she drew near me and said, "If I defeat you, I will do to you what I have done to these [people]." Then Abū Bakr cried and said, "I saw this [dream] before I came to Baghdad."[13] | 60

Al-Fuḍayl b. ʿIyāḍ said,

Ibn ʿAbbās رَضِيَٱللَّهُعَنْهُ said, "On the day of resurrection, this world will be brought forward in the form of a blind,[14] white-haired crone, who will bare her incisors. As she looks down on creation, it will be said, Do you recognize this one?"

[The people] will respond, "We seek refuge in God from recognizing this one!"

Then it will be said, "It is this world for which you slew one another, and broke familial bonds, and envied, and hated one another, and became deluded."

12 Ibn Abī l-Dunyā, *Dhamm al-dunyā*, 24–25 (no. 28).

13 Ibn Abī l-Dunyā, *Dhamm al-dunyā*, 25 (no. 30).

14 "Blind" (*zarqāʾ*) refers to a gray or blue opacity of the lens of the eyes, as occurs with cataracts. See Lane, *An Arabic-English Lexicon*, 3:1228 (s.v. ز - ر - ق). Cf. Q. 20:102.

Then she will be cast into hell and will call out, "Oh Lord! Where are my followers and my partisans?"

Then God عَزَّوَجَلَّ will say, "Join her, [you who] followed her and her partisans."[15]

Al-Fuḍayl [also] said,

"It has reached me that a man's spirit was taken up [in a dream], when suddenly [there appeared to him] a woman in the middle of the path, adorned with every [manner of] trinkets and clothing. No one could pass by her without her wounding him. And when she turned away, it was the best thing people had seen. When she turned back to face [them], it was the ugliest thing people had seen: a white-haired crone, bleary-eyed with glaucoma.

[The man] said, "I said, I seek refuge in God from you!"

She said, "No, by God. God will not protect you from me until you detest money."

I asked, "Who are you?"

She replied, "I am this world."[16]

Another example of this world and humanity's passage through it [follows]

Know that there are three states: [1] a state that has nothing in it from pre-eternity (*āzal*) until your existence; | [2] a state in which you are not in this world witnessing it, it is after your death until eternity (*ābad*); [3] and an intermediary state between pre-eternity and eternity, which are the days of your life in this world. So consider how long [your life] is in relation to the two ends [between] pre-eternity and eternity so that you might know that it is even shorter than a brief stopping point in a prolonged journey. 61

15 Ibn Abī l-Dunyā, *Dhamm al-dunyā*, 66–67 (no. 123).

16 Ibn Abī l-Dunyā, *Dhamm al-dunyā*, 67 (no. 124).

And [about] this [the Prophet] ﷺ said,

> What have I to do with this world? The similitude of me and this world is simply like that of a rider who set out on a summer day. A tree appeared before him, so he took a nap in its shade for a little while and then he departed and left it.[17]

Whoever views this world from this perspective would never rely on [this world] and would never be concerned by how his days have passed, whether in adversity and destitution or in abundance and comfort. In fact, he would not set a brick on [another] brick. The Messenger of God ﷺ passed away having never placed a brick on [another] brick nor a reed on [another] reed.[18]

He saw one of the Companions building a hut out of reeds, so he said, "I can only view the matter | as more pressing than that," and he renounced that [act].[19]

62

Jesus عَلَيْهِ السَّلَام alluded to something similar when he said, "This world is a bridge, so cross it and do not build on it."[20]

This is a clear example, for the life of this world is a crossing point to the hereafter. The cradle is the first incline onto the start of the bridge, while the grave is the second decline [to the exit]. Between the two is a fixed distance. There are people who have traversed half of the bridge, those who have traversed one-third of it, those who

17 Cf. al-Tirmidhī, *Sunan*, 4:588–589 (no. 2377); Ibn Mājah, *Sunan*, 2:1376 (no. 4109).

18 Al-Ṭabarānī relates a *ḥadīth* in his *al-Muʿjam al-awsaṭ* on the authority of ʿĀʾisha رَضِيَ اللَّهُ عَنْهَا, who said that the Messenger of God ﷺ said, "Whoever would ask about me or take pleasure in looking at me, let him look on one who is disheveled, emaciated, and striving… [One who] never placed a brick on another nor a reed on another. A standard was raised for him, and he took himself to it. Today is the training grounds, tomorrow is the race, and the destination is heaven or the fire." Al-Ṭabarānī, *al-Muʿjam al-awsaṭ*, 3:306–307 (no. 3241). Ibn Abī l-Dunyā also related a tradition from ʿUmar b. ʿAbd al-ʿAzīz, who refused to construct an edifice, saying, "The *sunna* of the Prophet is better than this world and all that is in it. He never constructed an edifice and never placed a brick on another nor a reed on another." Ibn Abī l-Dunyā, *Qiṣar al-amal*, 208 (no. 339).

19 This is meant to emphasize that doing good deeds is more important than superficialities. Al-Tirmidhī, *Sunan*, 4:568 (no. 2335); cf. Abū Dāwūd, *Sunan*, 5:252 (no. 5235). In the latter version of the *ḥadīth*, the Prophet was passing by ʿAbdallāh b. ʿAmr, who was mortaring a wall for himself with his mother. This alludes to decorating the wall with mortar, not repair work that is essential for upkeep [eds.].

20 Abū Ṭālib al-Makkī, *Qūt al-qulūb*, 1:256. Cf. Ibn Abī l-Dunyā, *Dhamm al-dunyā*, 26 (no. 33).

have traversed two-thirds of it, and those who have but a single step remaining and are unaware. However it may be, crossing it is inevitable. So building on the bridge and decorating it with [all] types of adornments while you are crossing it is the epitome of ignorance and [leads to] disappointment.

Another example of this world [is] in the tenderness of its commencement and the harshness of its completion

Know that the preliminary matters of this world seem to be easy and gentle. The [one who] engages in [this world] thinks that the pleasure of [first] diving into it is like the pleasure of being engrossed in it. How wrong! For plunging into this world is easy, while leaving it unscathed is difficult.

ʿAli [b. Abī Ṭālib رَضِيَ ٱللَّهُ عَنْهُ] wrote to Salmān al-Fārisī رَضِيَ ٱللَّهُ عَنْهُ with an example of this, | saying, 63

> The example of this world is like that of the serpent: it is smooth to the touch and its venom is deadly. So turn away from whatever appeals to you of [this world], for little of it will accompany you [into the hereafter]. Relinquish all your worries over it, for you have been assured of your departure from it. So be more cautious in it than you are happy, for whenever the companion [of this world] feels secure enough in it to find happiness, something loathsome pulls him away from it. Peace.[21]

21 Ibn Abī l-Dunyā, *Dhamm al-dunyā*, 44 (no. 74).

Another example of this world is [how] unfeasible it is to escape [from] its consequences after [one is] engrossed in it

The Messenger of God صَلَّى ٱللَّٰهُ عَلَيْهِ وَسَلَّمَ said, "The example of the adherent of this world (*ṣāḥib al-dunyā*) is [simply] like one who walks in water. Can one who walks in water keep his feet from getting wet?"[22]

This [*ḥadīth*] informs you [about] the ignorance of a people who think that they can engross [themselves] in the comforts of this world with their bodies, and keep their hearts pure of it and sever their connections to their inner states. This is one of Satan's ruses. Rather, were they taken from their [present state of comfort], they would be most tormented when they are separated from it. Thus, just as walking in water inevitably necessitates that water adheres to the foot [i.e., makes it wet], so too close association with [lit., wearing] this world necessitates attachment and darkness in [one's] heart. In fact, the attachment of the heart to this world prevents [one] from finding pleasure in worship.

Jesus عَلَيْهِ ٱلسَّلَامُ said,

64

> I tell you in truth: Just as the sick person looks at | food and takes no pleasure in it [because of] the severity of his pain, so too the adherent of this world does not enjoy worship and does not find pleasure in it like he finds in the love of this world. I tell you in truth: If the riding beast is not ridden and put to use, it becomes ornery and its manner changes. So, too, if hearts are not softened through the remembrance of death and the effort of worship, they harden and become tough. I tell you in truth: The wineskin, as long as it is not pierced and does not dry out, could be, undoubtedly, [i.e., as easily] a vessel for honey. So, too, hearts, as long as desires do not pierce them, avarice does not sully them, and comforts do wear them down, will become vessels of wisdom.[23]

---

22 Ibn Abī l-Dunyā, *Dhamm al-dunyā*, 51–52 (no. 89); al-Bayhaqī, *Shuʿab al-īmān*, 13:154–155 (no. 10099). In both sources Ḥasan reports the *ḥadīth* indirectly (*balāghan*) from the Prophet. For a similarly worded *ḥadīth* that is transmitted on the authority of Anas رَضِيَ ٱللَّٰهُ عَنْهُ to Ḥasan, cf. al-Bayhaqī, *Shuʿab al-īmān*, 13:73–74 (no. 9973); al-Bayhaqī, *Kitāb al-zuhd al-kabīr*, 136 (no. 257).

23 Ibn Abī l-Dunyā, *Dhamm al-dunyā*, 52 (no. 90).

Our Prophet ﷺ said,

> All that remains of this world is affliction and strife, and the example of the deeds of any one of you is like that of the vessel, if its upper part is good, its lower part is good, and if its upper part is bad, its lower part is bad.[24]

[Here is] another example, in addition to what preceded it, of what remains of this world and its paltriness

Anas said, "The Messenger of God ﷺ said, 'The example of this world is like that of a garment that has been torn [from use] from top to bottom and is held together by a thread at its bottom, and that thread is about to break.'"[25] | 65

[Here is] another example of [how] the attachments of this world lead one by one to destruction

Jesus عَلَيْهِ السَّلَامُ said, "The example of the one who seeks this world is like that of the one who drinks sea water: the more he drinks, the more [his] thirst increases until it kills him."[26]

24 Ibn Ḥanbal, *Musnad*, 28:66 (no. 16853). Cf. Ibn Mājah, *Sunan*, 2:1404–1405 (no. 4199), in which the first clause is missing.

25 Ibn Abī l-Dunyā, *Dhamm al-dunyā*, 107 (no. 221); Abū Nuʿaym, *Ḥilya*, 8:131; al-Bayhaqī, *Shuʿab al-īmān*, 12:470–471 (no. 9759).

26 Ibn Abī l-Dunyā, *Dhamm al-dunyā*, 146 (no. 342); al-Dīnawarī, *al-Majālisa wa-jawāhir al-ʿilm*, 246 (no. 1418).

[Here is] another example of [how] the end stage of this world contradicts its beginning, and a healthy commencement [contradicts] its harmful consequences

Know that the desires of the heart in this world are delectable, just like the desires for food by the stomach. At the time of death the servant will find that his desires for this world in his heart [have become] loathing, [disgust at] the stench, and ugliness, like he finds that delicious foods when they reach [their place] at the end of his stomach [i.e., fully digested]. Similarly, the food that was more delicious and more rich, and sweeter, is [more] disgusting and more putrid when he regurgitates it. Likewise every desire in the heart is most desirable, delectable, and strongly felt, [then becomes] more foul, more repugnant, more hated, and more harmful at the time of death. In fact, this is observable in this world. For whoever has had his home plundered and his spouse, child, and property taken [knows that] his misfortune, pain, and anguish over what he lost is commensurate with his [prior] enjoyment of it and his love and desire for it [in this world]. Thus, whatever he had that was most desirable and delectable when it was present is more calamitous and bitter on being lost. And death means [nothing] except the loss of what is in this world.

It has been related that the Prophet صَلَّى ٱللَّٰهُ عَلَيْهِ وَسَلَّمَ said to al-Ḍaḥḥāk b. Sufyān | al-Kilābī,

66

> "Is your food not brought to you salted and seasoned, and after it you drink milk and water?"
>
> He replied, "Yes, it is."
>
> [The Prophet] said, "Then what becomes of it?"
>
> He replied, "[It becomes] you-know-what, Messenger of God."
>
> He said, "God عَزَّ وَجَلَّ has set an example of this world in what becomes of the food of the son of Adam."[27]

Abī b. Kaʿb said, "The Messenger of God صَلَّى ٱللَّٰهُ عَلَيْهِ وَسَلَّمَ said, 'This world was set as an example for the son of Adam, so look at what

27 Ibn Ḥanbal, *Musnad*, 25:24–25 (no. 15747); cf. al-Ṭabarānī, *al-Muʿjam al-kabīr*, 8:358–359 (no. 8138), which does not mention that the food is salted and seasoned.

comes out of the son of Adam, though he may have seasoned and salted it [when it was food]. What becomes of it?'"[28]

The Prophet صَلَّى ٱللَّٰهُ عَلَيْهِ وَسَلَّمَ said, "God set this world as an example for the food of the son of Adam, and He has set the food of the son of Adam—though he may have seasoned and salted it—as an example for this world." Ḥasan [al-Baṣrī] said, "I saw them seasoning it with spices and scents, and then they cast it [away] as you observed."[29]

God عَزَّ وَجَلَّ has said, *Then let man look at his food* [Q. 80:24], [about which] Ibn ʿAbbās said, "to his excrement."[30]

A man said to Ibn ʿUmar,

> "I want to ask you something, but I feel embarrassed."
>
> [Ibn ʿUmar] said, | "Do not be shy, ask."
>
> He said, "Whenever one of us relieves himself and then stands, should he look at what [came out] of him?"
>
> He replied, "Yes. The angel says to him, 'Take a look, this is what you were greedy for. Look at what has become of it.'"[31]

67

Bushayr b. Kaʿb would say, "Come along so I can show you this world." He would take them to a dunghill and say, "Look at their fruits, their poultry, their honey, and their ghee [i.e., clarified butter]."[32]

28 Ibn al-Mubārak, *Zuhd*, 169 (no. 494).

29 Here Ḥasan alludes to the way food passes through the stomach and is excreted. Ibn al-Mubārak, *Zuhd*, 169–170 (no. 495); al-Bayhaqī, *Shuʿab al-īmān*, 7:448–449 (no. 5264).

30 Ibn Abī l-Dunyā, *al-Tawāḍuʿ wa-l-khumūl*, 204–205 (no. 213).

31 Al-Zabīdī refers to Abū Ṭālib al-Makkī, *Qūt al-qulūb*, see al-Zabīdī, *Itḥāf*, 8:112. Elsewhere Abū Ṭālib al-Makkī writes, "We have similarly related [a report] on the interpretation of God's تَعَالَىٰ words, *And in yourselves. Then will you not see?* [Q. 51:21]: 'It has been said [that this means] the places of excrement and urine.'" Abū Ṭālib al-Makkī, *Qūt al-qulūb*, 1:244.

32 Al-Zabīdī refers to Abū Ṭālib al-Makkī, *Qūt al-qulūb*, al-Zabīdī, *Itḥāf*, 8:113.

[Here is] another example of [how] this world compares with the hereafter

The Messenger of God ﷺ said, "This world [in comparison to] the hereafter is like one who dips his finger into the sea; look at what comes back to him."[33]

Another example of this world and its people [can be found] in their preoccupation with the comforts of this world, their heedlessness of the hereafter, and their enormous sorrow because of it

Know that the example of the people of this world, in their heedlessness, is like a group of people who have boarded a ship, and it has brought | them to an island. The captain has ordered them to disembark so they can relieve themselves, and he has warned them about lingering and has filled them with fear about the ship's departure and [has said that they should] be quick. So they dispersed to various parts of the island. Some of them relieved themselves and rushed back to the ship. They found the place [on the ship] empty, and chose the widest, softest, and most agreeable of spaces.

68

Some of them tarried on the island to gaze at its wondrous blossoms and flowers, its twisting thickets, and [to hear] the pleasant songs of its birds and their strangely balanced melodies. They began to observe its soil, stones, gemstones, and minerals of varying colors and shapes, beautiful in appearance, wonderfully decorated, and [these] wrest the gaze of the beholders with the beauty of their ornamentation and the wonder of their forms. Then they became mindful of the imminent danger of the ship's departure, and so they returned to it but did not find anything but a tight and narrow space into which they settled themselves.

Some of them dedicated themselves to [the island's] shells and stones. Delighted by their beauty, they could not let themselves leave them behind, so they took a bunch with them. They did not find on

33 Muslim, *Ṣaḥīḥ*, 4:2193 (no. 2858).

the ship anything but a tight space, while their load of stones made it even tighter. [The stones] became a burden and a curse, and they regretted taking them. They were unwilling to toss them, nor could they find a place to set them down in the ship, so they carried them on their backs [lit., on their neck]. They were sorry to have taken them, but this sorrow did nothing for them.

Some of them went deep into the [island's] thickets and forgot about the boat. They ventured far off in their wandering and pleasure seeking until the captain's calls no longer reached them, as they were preoccupied with eating the [island's] fruit, smelling its blossoms, and enjoying its trees. All the while they were terrified of | 69 predators and prone to slips and falls. They could not escape briars sticking into their clothes, branches wounding their bodies, thorns penetrating their feet, a frightening noise instilling them with terror, and thorn bushes tearing their clothes and exposing their nakedness, [thus] preventing them from leaving even if they wanted to. When the calls of the ship's people reached some of them, they departed, laden with all that they carried. They did not find space in the boat, so they remained on the shore until they starved to death. Some of them did not hear the calls, and the ship set off. Some of them were seized by the [island's] predators, some of them got lost and wandered about aimlessly until they perished, and some of them died in the [island's] quagmires, while some of them were bitten by serpents. They were scattered about like rotting corpses.

As for the one who arrived at the boat burdened by all of the flowers and decorative stones that he had grabbed, he was made a slave to [these things]. He was filled with sorrow at having kept them while also filled with fear of losing them. The space around him had grown tight, and before long the flowers withered, the color of the stones grew dull, and their putrid smell became apparent. Thus, in addition to constricting him, they [became] harmful to him with their noxious repugnant [fumes] and he was left with no recourse but to throw them into the sea to escape them. But he was effected by what he had already consumed of them. Before he could reach his homeland, sickness from these fumes became apparent in him, and so he arrived diseased and sickened.

The one who returned promptly only lost out on the spaciousness of his place [on the ship]. So he was harmed by the tightness of this space for a time, but when he arrived at his homeland he rested.

The one who returned first found the widest space for himself and arrived at his homeland sound. | 70

This is an example of the types of people of this world, their preoccupations with their fleeting fortunes, their forgetfulness of their commencement and completion [in this world] and their heedlessness of the end result of their affair. How vile is it for [one who] claims to be insightful and intelligent, that he should be deceived by stones from the earth—gold and silver, and by dry plant stalks, the beauty of this world—while nothing of this sort will accompany him after death! Rather these [things] will become a burden and a curse for him, while they fill him with sorrow and fear. Such is the state of all people, save for whomever God تَعَالَىٰ safeguards.

[Here is] another example of people deluded by this world and the weakness of their belief in God's تَعَالَىٰ word that warns them of the calamities of this world

Ḥasan [al-Baṣrī] رَحِمَهُ ٱللَّهُ said, it has reached me that the Messenger of God صَلَّى ٱللَّهُ عَلَيْهِ وَسَلَّمَ said to his Companions,

> "My example and your example and the example this world is [like] the parable of a people who set out into a dusty desert until they exhaust their provisions, as they did not know how far they would be traveling nor how much [of the desert] remained. With their backs bare,[34] they remained in the middle of the desert with no provisions and no cargo and so grew certain of [their] annihilation. Such was their state when suddenly there [appeared] advancing toward them a man who was fully dressed with his head dripping [i.e., with oil or water]."

34 This alludes to the death of their riding mounts; al-Zabīdī, *Itḥāf*, 8:114.

They said, "This [man] is fresh from fertile country, and he would not come to you unless it were nearby."

When he reached them he said, "You there."

They replied, "You there."

He said, "What is your situation?"

They replied, "As you see."

He said, "What do you think you would do if I were to guide you to fresh water and verdant gardens?" | 71

They replied, "We would not disobey you in anything."

He said, "[Give me] your vows and covenants in God's [name]."

So they gave him their vows and covenants in God's [name] to not disobey him in anything.

[The Prophet] said, "He then brought them to fresh water and verdant gardens, and he stayed with them as God willed."

Then he said, "You there."

They replied, "You there."

He said, "Time to leave."

They said, "To where?"

He said, "To water that is not like your water [here] and to gardens that are not like your gardens [here]."

The majority of them said, "By God! We did not find this place, to the point that we thought we would never find it. What would we do with a life better than this?"

[The Prophet] said,

A minority group among them said, "Did you not give this man your vows and your covenants in God's [name], to not disobey him in anything? He proved himself truthful to you with his first statements, and by God, he will prove himself truthful to you again in the end."

[The guide] then left along with those who followed him, while the rest of them stayed behind. An enemy suddenly descended on [the majority that stayed behind], and they were made captive or killed.[35]

[Here is] another example of peoples' [enjoyment of] luxury in this world and then their anguish over their separation from it

Know that the example of people in what they were given of this world is like that of a man who tidies up his home and decorates it, and invites groups of people into his home successively, one after another. Then a person enters his home and is presented with a golden tray with incense and scents for him to smell and leave for the next person, not for him to possess and take with him. [But] being ignorant of this injunction, he thought that the tray had been gifted to him, and so his heart grew attached to it | when he thought it was his. When it was taken from him, he was grieved and anguished. The one who was knowledgeable of [the host's] injunction benefited from [the tray] and thanked [the host]. He returned it with a good heart and open chest [i.e., without any hard feelings].

72

Similarly, whoever recognizes God's precedent in this world knows that it is an abode of [temporary] hospitality—allocated to those who are passing through and not to those who take up residency—so that [those passing through] can provision themselves from it and avail themselves of what it contains, just like travelers avail themselves of loans.[36] They do not turn their hearts in full toward them [the rentals], so they will not [suffer] when it is time to leave [them].

These then are examples of this world and its perils and calamities. We ask God تعالى, the Sublime and All-Knowing, for fitting assistance from His generosity and clemency.

---

35 Ibn Abī l-Dunyā, *Dhamm al-dunyā*, 50–51 (no. 88), on the authority of Ḥasan who heard it indirectly (*balāghan*) from the Prophet. Cf. Ibn Ḥanbal, *Musnad*, 4:227–228 (no. 2402); al-Ṭabarānī, *al-Muʿjam al-kabīr*, 12:219 (no. 12940) where the *ḥadīth* is reported by Ibn ʿAbbās رضي الله عنهما. It recounts a similar dream vision of the Prophet صلى الله عليه وسلم in which the man who appears to guide the group is explicitly equated with the Prophet.

36 Loans (*ʿawārī*) refer to the rental of rooms and sometimes animals for journeys (just as we rent cars and hotel rooms today) [eds.].

4

An Elucidation of the Reality and Essence of This World Regarding the Servant

73

Know that to recognize that this world is censured will not suffice you as long as you do not recognize what is actually blameworthy in this world, what ought to be avoided in it, and what is not to be avoided. Thus, it is necessary for us to clarify what is blameworthy in this world and [what it is] compulsory to avoid, as it is an enemy lying in wait on God's تَعَالَىٰ path.

So we say, your worldly [life] and your hereafter are terms to designate two states of your heart: the near and close one of them is called "world" (*dunyā*), which is everything before death, while the later and delayed one [the second] is called "hereafter" (*ākhira*) which is what comes after death. Then all of your share, goals, allotments, desires, and enjoyment in the present state before death is this world with respect to you.

Except, everything that you incline to, including your allotment and share, is not blameworthy; rather, [it falls into one of] three divisions.

The first division is whatever accompanies you into the hereafter and whose fruits remain with you after death. This is two things only: knowledge and deeds.

By knowledge I mean knowledge of God, His attributes, His acts, His angels, His books, His messengers, and the kingdom of His earth and His heaven; and knowledge of the law (*sharīʿa*) of His Prophet صَلَّى ٱللَّٰهُ عَلَيْهِ وَسَلَّمَ.

By deeds I mean worship done purely for the countenance of God تَعَالَىٰ. | 74

The scholar might rejoice in knowledge until it becomes the most pleasurable thing for him. He thus forsakes sleep, marriage, and food in the enjoyment of it, as for him it is more desirable than all of these. [Knowledge] has thus become [his] immediate gain in this world. However, when we refer to the blameworthy in this world, we would not consider this [knowledge] to be part of this world in essence; rather, we would say that [knowledge] is part of the hereafter.

Similarly, the worshiper might rejoice in his worship and find pleasure in it to the extent that, were he deprived of it, this would be the severest of punishments for him. Someone even said, "I do not fear death except in that it will come between me and my standing [in prayer] at night."[1]

Another [person] used to say [in supplication], "Oh God! Grant me the power to pray, bow, and prostrate in the grave!"[2] Thus, the prayer became one of this person's immediate gains, and every immediate gain is labeled "this world" (*al-dunyā*) in that it is derived from *dunūw* (proximity). However, by this we do not mean [that it is] blameworthy in this world.

[The Prophet] صَلَّى ٱللَّٰهُ عَلَيْهِ وَسَلَّمَ said, "Three things of this world of yours have been made beloved to me: fragrance, women, and the coolness of my eye in prayer."[3] Thus, he has placed prayer in the

---

1 I.e., *qiyām al-layl*. Abū Nuʿaym relates a statement of Abū Sulaymān al-Dārānī, who said, "Worry [over the hereafter] is more delightful to the people of obedience than is diversion to the people of whimsy. If it were not for the night [for standing in prayer], they would not want to stay in this world." Abū Nuʿaym, *Ḥilya*, 9:275.

2 Thābit al-Bunānī used to supplicate, "Oh God! If you were ever to allow someone to pray in his grave, then allow Thābit to pray in his grave." Abū Nuʿaym, *Ḥilya*, 2:319.

3 The "coolness of my eye" refers to the Prophet's state of tranquility when engaged in prayer. Al-Nasāʾī, *Sunan*, 7:61 (no. 3939); Ibn Ḥanbal, *Musnad*, 19:307 (no. 12294). Neither source includes the words "three things" in its narration of the *ḥadīth*. For the wording of the *ḥadīth* used by the author here, see Abū Ṭālib al-Makkī, *Qūt al-qulūb*, 2:249. In his *Talkhīṣ al-ḥabīr*, al-ʿAsqalānī writes, "It has become common usage to add 'three things' [to this *ḥadīth*]. Abū Bakr Ibn Fūrak commented on this in a volume devoted to the subject, and al-Ghazālī has similarly mentioned it in his *Iḥyāʾ*, though we have not found the words 'three things' in any of the [*ḥadīth*'s] reliable lines of transmission." Al-ʿAsqalānī, *al-Talkhīṣ al-ḥabīr*, 5:2155.

class of the enjoyments of "this world." | This is because everything that pertains to sensory perception and visual observation is from the realm of what is seen (*ʿālam al-shahāda*), which is part of this world. Finding enjoyment in moving one's limbs during bowing and prostration can only [take place] in this world, and for that reason, [the Messenger] attributed it to this world. In this book, on the other hand, we only object to the blameworthy in this world, and so we say that this is not part of "this world." 75

The second division—the [first division's] extreme opposite—is everything in which there is an immediate gain that bears no fruit whatsoever in the hereafter. [These are things] such as finding enjoyment in any act of disobedience, or luxuriating in permissible things that are beyond the scope of necessities and [basic] needs and pertain to the life of comfort and frivolity. Examples [include] luxuriating in *heaped-up sums of gold and silver, fine branded horses, cattle, tilled land* [Q. 3:14], male and female slaves, horses, livestock, palaces, mansions, fine apparel, and delectable foods. The share of the servant in all such things is [considered part of] the blameworthy in this world, and careful consideration should go into anything that is deemed superfluous or needed only in extenuating circumstances, as it has been related by ʿUmar رَضِيَ اللهُ عَنْهُ that he appointed Abū l-Dardāʾ as governor of Homs. [The latter] had taken to using a shed that he had spent two dirhams on, so ʿUmar wrote to him, "From ʿUmar b. al-Khaṭṭāb, commander of the faithful, to ʿUwaymir:[4] | The buildings of Persia and Rome are sufficient [to not] build [anything else] in this world when God has proclaimed its ruin. So, once my letter reaches you, I dispatch you and your family to Damascus."[5] He then

The editor of the Minhāj edition of the *Iḥyāʾ* writes, "Assuming that the words did not originally exist, what the author mentions here still holds, as he explicitly and categorically rejects [the idea that] prayer is part of the hereafter."

4 Abū l-Dardāʾ's first name was ʿUwaymir. See al-Dhahabī, *Siyar*, 2:335.

5 Ibn Abī l-Dunyā, *Qiṣar al-amal*, 172–173 (no. 266); al-Bayhaqī, *Shuʿab al-īmān*, 13:235 (no. 10251).

remained [in Damascus] until he died. [ʿUmar] thus considered this [shed] to be something superfluous in this world, so reflect on that.

The third division—between the two extremes—is every immediate gain that assists in [good] deeds for the hereafter, such as the ration of food for basic sustenance, the single coarse shirt [to clothe one's nakedness], and everything necessary for a person's survival and health, which [he uses to] attain knowledge and [do good] deeds. Like the first division, this is not part of this world because it is an aid and expedient to [the things of] the first division. Whatever the servant consumes with the intent [of using it] in the pursuance of knowledge and deeds does not make him a consumer of this world nor one of the children of this world. If his motive is [to attain] his immediate gain but [it is] not an aid to piety, [then the consumed thing] falls under the second division and becomes part of "this world."

Only three qualities remain with the servant on death: purity of heart (by which I mean that it is cleansed of the contaminants of this world), his intimacy with the remembrance of God تعالى, and his love of God تعالى. Purity of heart and the cleansing of it are only obtained by abstaining from the desires of this world. Intimacy | is only obtained by frequent and persistent remembrance of God تعالى. And love is only obtained by gnosis, while gnosis of God is only obtained by perpetual reflection. These three qualities are the means of deliverance and felicity after death—they are *the enduring good deeds* [Q. 18:46].

77

As for cleansing the heart of the desires of this world, this is a means of deliverance since it is a shield between the servant and God's torment, as it has been mentioned in the reports, "The servant's deeds will defend him [in the hereafter]. When torment comes from beneath him, his having stood at night in prayer will come to drive [it] away from him. When it comes from in front of him, his acts of charity will come to drive [it] away from him…" (the *ḥadīth* continues).[6]

As for intimacy and love, they are a means of felicity. They are the servant's conveyance to his pleasure in encountering and witnessing [God]. This felicity hastens everything that follows death up until the time comes to glimpse heaven. Then the grave becomes a garden from the gardens of heaven. How can the grave that surrounds him not be a garden from heaven when he only has a singular Beloved, while obstacles were hindering him from the perpetual intimacy of remembrance of Him and observation of His beauty?[7] These obstacles have been lifted, and he has been freed from [his] prison and has been left alone with his Beloved. Thus he has reached Him overjoyed, free from all hindrances, and secure from separation [from Him ever again]. | 78

How can the lover of this world not be tormented at the time of death when the only beloved he has is in this world? [That beloved] has been taken from him. They have been cut off from one another, and all schemes to return to [the beloved] have been stymied.

> What is the state of the person who had only one,
> And that one has been taken from him?[8]

Death is not a complete privation. It is merely a departure from the beloved things of this world and a procession to God تَعَالَىٰ.

Therefore, the wayfarer (*sālik*) along the path to the hereafter is the one who devotes himself to the means [to obtain] these three attributes. [These means] are the remembrance (*dhikr*) [of God], reflection (*fikr*) [on God], and the deeds that wean him off the

---

6 Cf. al-Ṭabarānī, *al-Aḥādīth al-ṭawāl*, 84–85 (no. 36); Ibn ʿAsākir, *Tārīkh madīnat Dimashq*, 34:406–407. Ibn Ḥanbal relates another *ḥadīth* on the authority of Asmāʾ, رَضِيَ اللَّهُ عَنْهَا who heard the Prophet say, "When a person enters his grave, if he were a believer, his acts of prayer and fasting surround him. The angel comes toward him from the direction of his prayer, which repels him, and from the direction of his fasting, which repels him…" (the *ḥadīth* continues). Ibn Ḥanbal, *Musnad*, 44:535–536 (no. 26976).

7 Read *dawām al-uns* (perpetual intimacy) for *al-uns*, as accords with al-Zabīdī, *Itḥāf*, 8:119.

8 See al-Thaʿālibī, *al-Tamthīl*, 211. The meter of the poem is *sarīʿ*.

desires of this world, make the enjoyment of them odious to him, and inhibit him [lit., cut him off] from them. All of this is impossible except with a sound body, and a sound body is only attained with sustenance, clothing, and shelter. Each of these requires means. If the servant takes from this world the minimum amount that is necessary of these three things for the sake of his hereafter, he is not one of the children of this world. With respect to him, this world is a farm for the hereafter. If he takes [from this world] out of self-indulgence and with the intent of enjoying luxury, he has become one of the children of this world and one of those who covet its fortunes.

However, coveting worldly fortunes can be divided into [two categories]: that which exposes its adherent to torment in the hereafter (which is called unlawful), and that which bars [its adherent] from the highest stations [of heaven] and exposes him to a protracted reckoning (which is called lawful). The person of insight knows that 79 a protracted | standing on the plains of resurrection for reckoning is also a torment, for "whoever is scrutinized in [his] reckoning will be tormented."[9] The Messenger of God ﷺ said, "[what] is lawful is reckoned, and [what] is unlawful is a torment."[10] He also said, "[what] is lawful is a torment," though it will be a torment that is lighter than the torment of unlawful [acts]. In fact, even if there were no reckoning, everything from the highest stations of heaven that slips away—and the grief that manifests in one's heart on [seeing] it slip away on account of [worldly] fortunes that are paltry, despicable, and ephemeral—that too is a torment. Compare this to your own state in this world, as you look at your peers who have outdone you in worldly happiness—how your heart breaks with grief over them! [This] is in spite of your knowledge that these are expiring and ephemeral joys that are spoiled by impurities that have no clarity. What then of your state if you pass [an opportunity] for felicity, the sublimity of which defies description and which would not cease [despite] the passage of time.

9 These words are related in a *ḥadīth*. See Muslim, *Ṣaḥīḥ*, 4:2204 (no. 2876); al-Bukhārī, *Ṣaḥīḥ*, 8:111 (no. 6536).

10 Al-Daylamī, *Musnad al-firdaws*, 5:283 (no. 8192), on the authority of Ibn ʿAbbās رضي الله عنهما.

So everyone who enjoys luxury in this world—by hearing a bird's song, or gazing on greenery, or sipping cool water—diminishes his share in the hereafter many times over. This is the intended meaning of [the Prophet's] صَلَّى ٱللَّهُ عَلَيْهِ وَسَلَّمَ words to ʿUmar رَضِيَ ٱللَّهُ عَنْهُ, "This is one of the [worldly] comforts that you will be questioned about" (referring here to cool water).[11] Being subjected to questioning [before God] | 80 brings with it disgrace, fear, peril, distress, and waiting. These are all things that diminish one's share [of paradise]. For this reason ʿUmar رَضِيَ ٱللَّهُ عَنْهُ said, "Release me from its reckoning," when he was thirsty, and cool water with honey was offered to him. He turned it with his hand and then refrained from drinking it.[12]

Be it meager or plentiful, lawful or unlawful, this world is cursed, except for what helps in [cultivating] the fear (*taqwā*) of God—that amount of it is not [considered] part of "this world." The stronger and more certain anyone's realization of this is, the more wary he is of the comforts of this world. Even Jesus عَلَيْهِ ٱلسَّلَامُ laid his head on a stone when he slept and then tossed it away when Satan appeared before him and told him, "You have coveted this world."[13]

And even Solomon عَلَيْهِ ٱلسَّلَامُ, in his kingdom, would feed his people the most delicious foods, while he would eat barley bread.[14] In this manner, he used his kingdom as a test of his soul and an ordeal, as patient self-restraint from delicious foods is more taxing when they are at hand and one has access to them.

11 Al-Nasāʾī, *Sunan*, 6:246 (no. 3640); Ibn Ḥanbal, *Musnad*, 23:8 (no. 14637); al-Bayhaqī, *Shuʿab al-īmān*, 6:327 (no. 4279).

12 Ibn Ḥanbal, *al-Zuhd*, 99 (no. 628). Ibn Abī Shayba relates a report on the authority of Bukayr b. ʿAtīq, who said, "I once gave Saʿīd b. Jubayr a drink with some honey in a cup. He drank it and then said, 'By God! I will certainly be questioned about this.' So I asked, 'Why?' He replied, 'I drank it and took pleasure in it.'" Ibn Abī Shayba, *al-Muṣannaf*, 19:405–406 (no. 36492).

13 Cf. Ibn Abī l-Dunyā, *Kitāb al-zuhd*, 210 (no. 557); Ibn ʿAsākir, *Tārīkh madīnat Dimashq*, 47:416.

14 See Ibn Ḥanbal, *al-Zuhd*, 76 (no. 466).

[About] this, God تَعَالَىٰ removed this world from our Prophet صَلَّى ٱللَّٰهُ عَلَيْهِ وَسَلَّمَ, and so he went hungry | for several days,[15] and he tied the stone over his belly out of hunger.[16]

81

[About] this, God set affliction and tribulations on His prophets and saints and then on those next in status and so on.[17] This is all out of consideration for them—and is a blessing for them—so that their share of the hereafter might be plentiful. Similarly, the compassionate father prohibits his son from enjoying fruit and forces him [to experience] the pain of blood-letting and cupping[18] out of benevolence toward him and love for him, not out of greed [i.e., to have more for himself].

You know from this that everything that is not for God is part of this world, while everything that is for God عَزَّوَجَلَّ is not part of this world.

If you were to ask: What then is for God سُبْحَانَهُ?

I would respond: Things [fall] into three divisions.

---

15 Al-Tirmidhī and Ibn Mājah relate a *ḥadīth* on the authority of Ibn ʿAbbās رَضِيَ ٱللَّٰهُ عَنْهُمَا, who said, "The Messenger of God would spend several consecutive nights hungry, while his family had no supper. And usually their bread was barley bread." Al-Tirmidhī, *Sunan*, 4:580 (no. 2360); Ibn Mājah, *Sunan*, 2:1111 (no. 3347). As for God's سُبْحَانَهُ removing this world from [the Prophet] صَلَّى ٱللَّٰهُ عَلَيْهِ وَسَلَّمَ, it comes in multiple reports, including what al-Bukhārī and Muslim relate on the authority of ʿUmar رَضِيَ ٱللَّٰهُ عَنْهُ, who said to the Prophet صَلَّى ٱللَّٰهُ عَلَيْهِ وَسَلَّمَ, "This mat has left marks on the side of your body, while I see only a few things in your cupboard. The emperors of Rome and Persia [live] among orchards and rivers, while you are God's Messenger and chosen one, and yet your cupboard [looks like] this?" [The Prophet] said, "Oh son of al-Khaṭṭāb! Are you not satisfied that we have the hereafter and they have this world?" Al-Bukhārī, *Ṣaḥīḥ*, 3:133–135 (no. 2468); Muslim, *Ṣaḥīḥ*, 2:1105–1108 (no. 1479).

16 See al-Bukhārī, *Ṣaḥīḥ*, 5:108 (no. 4101), where the Prophet's act is reported in the context of the Battle of the Trench (see page 40, n.7).

17 See, inter alia, Ibn Mājah, *Sunan*, 2:1334 (no. 4023); al-Tirmidhī, *Sunan*, 4:601–602 (no. 2398).

18 Cupping and blood-letting were commonly done for health reasons, even though they are painful they were thought to improve one's health [eds.].

[First] is whatever could not conceivably be for God عَزَّوَجَلَّ, which are those things designated as disobedience, | prohibited [actions], and all types of luxury in permissible [things]. This is the blameworthy portion of this world in its absolute [sense]; it is this world in form and meaning. 82

[Second] is what is for God in its [outward] form, though it may be done for other than God. This [covers] three [things]: reflection [on God], remembrance [of God], and abstaining from desires. If these three are performed in private and with the only motive behind them being [the fulfillment] of God's command and [the desire for] the hereafter, then they are for God and are not part of this world. If the objective of one's reflection on God is to seek knowledge for the sake of self-aggrandizement and to seek acceptance from people by showing off one's knowledge, or if the objective of abstaining from one's desire is to save money, or to protect the health of one's body, or to gain renown for one's asceticism, then [these acts] become part of this world by definition, even if—in their [outward] form—they are thought to be for God تَعَالَىٰ.

[Third] is what is, in its [outward] form self-indulgent, though in its signification it can be done for God سُبْحَانَهُ. These [are things] like eating, marriage, and everything connected to one's survival and the survival of [one's] children. If one's intent [in an action] is self-indulgence, then it is part of this world. If one's intent is to use it for piety (*taqwā*), then it is for God by definition even if it takes the [outward] form of this world. The [Prophet] صَلَّىٱللَّهُعَلَيْهِوَسَلَّمَ said, "Whoever lawfully seeks this world to show off and compete with others, he will meet God who is angry with him. Whoever seeks it to avoid begging and safeguard his soul, he will appear on the day of resurrection with his face like the full moon."[19] Notice how this varies according to intent. | 83

Therefore, this world is your immediate self-indulgence that is unnecessary with regard to the hereafter. This is designated as passion, which He تَعَالَىٰ alluded to with His words, [*As for he who...*]

19 For a similar *ḥadīth* narrated on the authority of Abū Hurayra رَضِيَٱللَّهُعَنْهُ, see Ibn Abī l-Dunyā, *al-ʿIyyāl*, 111 (no. 32); Ibn Abī Shayba, *al-Muṣannaf*, 11:379–380 (no. 22625); Abū Nuʿaym, *Ḥilya*, 3:109–110; al-Bayhaqī, *Shuʿab al-īmān*, 13:18 (no. 9890).

prevented his soul from [*unlawful*] *passion, indeed, heaven will be* [*his*] *refuge* [Q. 79:40–41].

Passions converge on five matters, which God تَعَالَىٰ summed up in His words: *The life of this world is but amusement and diversion and adornment and boasting to one another and competition in increase of wealth and children* [Q. 57:20]. These five things stem from seven entities, which are summed up in the words [of God] تَعَالَىٰ: *Beautified for people is the love of that which they desire—of women and sons, heaped-up sums of gold and silver, fine branded horses, and cattle and tilled land. That is the enjoyment of worldly life* [Q. 3:14].

So, you have come to know that everything that is for God is not part of this world, while the amount of food that is necessary and what is essential for shelter and clothing: this is for God if the intent is the countenance of God. Overdoing [such things] is a luxury, which is for other than God. Between luxury and necessity is a level that is designated as "need," which has two extremes and a middle portion. One extreme verges on necessity and is harmless if it is not possible to restrict oneself to the limit of necessity. Another extreme skews toward the side of luxury and verges on it. It should be treated with caution. Between the two [extremes] are middle points that resemble one another, and whoever circles what is forbidden almost falls into it. Prudence [here] is to be found in caution, fear of God (*taqwā*), and to the extent possible, [one should] approach the limit of necessity. [This is done] in emulation of the prophets—God's blessings be on them all—and the saints, as they would bring themselves back to the limit of necessity.

Even the family of Uways al-Qaranī thought that he was insane owing to the extreme limitations that he put on | himself. So they built a house for him at the door to their home, and one year, two years, and three years would pass them by without [them] seeing his face. He would leave [his house] at the first call [to *fajr*] and return after the final night prayer (*ʿishā*). For his food he would collect date stones. Whenever he came on some dry bread, he would save it for his breakfast. If he did not have enough to sustain him, he would sell his date stones and buy something to sustain him. His clothing was whatever he collected from the dunghills. He would thus collect rags, wash them in the Euphrates, stitch them together, and then

84

wear them. This was his clothing.[20] Sometimes he would pass by boys who would pelt him [with stones], thinking that he was insane. So he would say to them, "Brothers, if you must pelt me, then pelt me with small stones. For I am afraid that you will cause my heel to bleed, and the time for prayer will come, and I will be unable to find water."[21] Such was his conduct. Because of this, the Messenger of God ﷺ extolled him by saying, "I surely feel the breath of the All-Merciful coming from the direction of Yemen," which was an allusion to him رَحِمَهُ ٱللَّهُ.[22]

When ʿUmar b. al-Khaṭṭāb رَضِيَ ٱللَّهُ عَنْهُ was entrusted with the caliphate, he said, "Oh people! Whoever is an inhabitant of Iraq, stand up."

> [The narrator] said, "So they stood up." Then he said, "Everyone sit except for the inhabitants of Kufa." So they sat. Then he said, "Everyone sit except for those from Murād [clan]." So they sat. Then he said, "Everyone sit except for those of the Qaran [tribe]." So everyone sat except for a single man. | 85
>
> ʿUmar رَضِيَ ٱللَّهُ عَنْهُ said to him, "Are you a Qaranī?"
>
> He replied, "Yes."
>
> So [ʿUmar] asked, "Do you know Uways b. ʿĀmir al-Qaranī?" Then he described [Uways] to him.
>
> [The man] replied, "Yes. But, commander of the faithful, why are you asking about that one? By God! None of our people are more foolish than he is. None are more insane than he is. None are more destitute than he is. And none are lowlier than he is."
>
> ʿUmar رَضِيَ ٱللَّهُ عَنْهُ began to weep. Then he said, "I only said what I said because I heard the Messenger of God ﷺ saying, 'Through [Uways's] intercession, [even] the likes of the Rabīʿa and Muḍar tribes will enter [heaven].'"[23]

---

20 Ibn ʿAsākir, *Tārīkh madīnat Dimashq*, 9:431–432.

21 In some schools of Islamic law, bleeding (e.g., from a cut) a specific amount requires one to renew his ablutions [eds.]. Al-Qushayrī, *al-Risāla*, 412.

22 Al-Ṭabarānī, *al-Muʿjam al-kabīr*, 7:60 (no. 6357). Cf. Ibn Ḥanbal, *Musnad*, 16:576–577 (no. 10978), where the *ḥadīth* records "the breath of your Lord" in place of "the breath of the All-Merciful."

23 Ibn Abī Shayba relates a *ḥadīth* in his *Muṣannaf* on the authority of Ḥasan, who said, "The Messenger of God ﷺ said, 'Through the intercession of a man from my community, [even] the likes of the Rabīʿa and Muḍar tribes will enter

Harim b. Ḥayyān said,

"When I heard these words of ʿUmar b. al-Khaṭṭāb رَضِيَ ٱللَّهُ عَنْهُ, I went to Kufa—my only concern was to seek out Uways al-Qaranī and ask about him—until I stumbled on him sitting by the bank of the Euphrates around midday, making ablutions and washing his clothes." He continued, "I recognized him from the description given to me. There stood a fleshy man, of very dark complexion, with a shaved head, a thick beard, incredibly foul-smelling, [with an] ugly face, and dreadful appearance."

[Harim] said, "So, I greeted him with peace, and he returned the greeting and looked at me. Then I said, may God preserve you from any man! And I stretched out my hand to shake his, but he held back from shaking mine. I said, may God have mercy on you, Uways, and may he forgive you. God's mercy be on you, how are you? Tears were choking me, out of my love and pity for him when I saw what I saw of his state, to the point that I started to weep, and so did he.

He said, "God preserve you, Harim b. Ḥayyān. How are you, my brother? Who led you to me?"

I replied, "God."

To which he said, "There is no god but God! Glory be to God, *Indeed, the promise of our Lord has been fulfilled* [Q. 17:108]." | 86

[Harim] said, "I was astonished when he recognized me. And no, by God, I had never seen him before that, and he had never seen me. So I said, from where did you come to know

heaven.'" When Ḥasan was asked for the name of the man, he replied, "Uways al-Qaranī." Ibn Abī Shayba, *al-Muṣannaf*, 17:255–256 (no. 133009). Al-Tirmidhī also records a *ḥadīth* on the authority of Ḥasan, who reported that the Prophet said, "On the day of resurrection, ʿUthmān b. ʿAffān will intercede for [even] the likes of the Rabīʿa and Muḍar tribes." Al-Tirmidhī, *Sunan*, 4:627 (no. 2439). Al-Ṭabarānī related a *ḥadīth* on the authority of Abū Umāma, who said that the Prophet said, "Among the believers is a person through whose intercession [even] the likes of the Rabīʿa and Muḍar tribes will enter heaven." The person's name was not mentioned. Al-Ṭabarānī, *al-Muʿjam al-kabīr*, 8:280 (no. 7919). On the boorish qualities of the Rabīʿa and Muḍar tribes as juxtaposed with the faith of the people of Yemen, see, inter alia, al-Bukhārī, *Ṣaḥīḥ*, 7:53 (no. 5303).

my name and the name of my father, as I have never seen you before today, and you have never seen me?

He replied, "*I was informed by the All-Knowing, the All-Aware* [Q. 66:3]. My spirit recognized your spirit at the moment that my soul spoke with your soul. The spirits have souls similar to the souls of our bodies, and the believers recognize one another and love one another through the spirit of God, even if they never meet. They recognize one another and converse, though their homes may be distant and their dwellings may be separated."

[Harim] continued, "I said, let me hear a *ḥadīth* of the Messenger of God ﷺ from you, God's mercy be on you."

He said, "I did not reach the Messenger of God ﷺ while he was alive, and I did not have companionship with him—may my father and mother [be sacrificed] for the Messenger of God ﷺ. However, I once saw a man who had seen him, and he relayed his words to me that are similar to what was related to you. But, I have no desire to open this door on myself and be a *ḥadīth* narrator, nor a mufti or a judge. My soul is too occupied to be distracted by people, oh Harim b. Ḥayyān!"

So I [Harim] said, "My brother, recite to me some verses of God's book for me to hear, make supplications [to God] on my behalf, and give me sound counsel that I can take with me, for I love you deeply for the sake of God."

[Harim] said, "So, he stood up and led me by the hand to the bank of the Euphrates."

Then he said, "I seek refuge in God, the All-Hearing, the All-Knowing, from the accursed Satan..." Then he started to weep and said, "My Lord said, and the most veracious words are His, the most truthful narrations are His, and the most truthful speech is His..." Then he recited, "*And We did not create the heavens and earth and that between them in play. We did not create them except in truth, but most of them do not know* [Q. 44:38–39]... Until the point that | he reached His words, *Indeed, He is the Exalted in Might, the All-Compassionate* [Q.

87

44:42]." Then he let out a moan [that made] me think that he had fainted and said, "Oh son of Ḥayyān! Your father Ḥayyān died, while you are on the verge of death, and then it is off to heaven or hell. Your father Adam died. Your mother Eve died. Noah died. Abraham, the true friend of the All-Merciful, died. Moses, the secret interlocutor of the All-Merciful, died. David, the vicegerent of the All-Merciful, died. Muḥammad صَلَّى ٱللَّهُ عَلَيْهِ وَسَلَّمَ, the Messenger of the Lord of the worlds, died. Abū Bakr, the vicegerent of the Muslims, died. And ʿUmar b. al-Khaṭṭāb, my brother and best friend, died."

Then he said, "Oh ʿUmar! Oh ʿUmar!" [Harim continued], "I said, may God have mercy on you! ʿUmar has not died."

[Uways] replied, "My Lord informed me of his death, and my soul informed me too." Then he said, "It is as if you and I are already among the dead," and so he sent blessings on the Prophet صَلَّى ٱللَّهُ عَلَيْهِ وَسَلَّمَ and made quiet supplications.

Then [Uways] said, "This is my sound counsel to you, Harim b. Ḥayyān: [hold to] the book of God and to announcing the deaths of the righteous believers.[24] Yours and mine have already been announced to me. For as long as you live, you must not let the remembrance of death leave your heart for the blink of an eye. Warn your people, when you return to them, and counsel the entire community of Muslims (*umma*). And do not dare depart from the majority community (*jamāʿa*) by even a handspan. For [if you do], you will have left your *dīn* without knowing it, and you will enter the fire on the day of resurrection. Make supplications [to God] for me and for you."

Then he said, "Oh God! This one claims that he loves me for Your sake and that he visited me for Your sake. | Make his face familiar to me in heaven, and let him enter [my home] in Your abode, the abode of peace [paradise]. Protect him for as long

88

24 The editor of the Minhāj edition provides alternate wordings here from two other manuscripts. The first (MS أ) reads: "My sound counsel to you is to remember God تَعَالَىٰ, to send blessings on the Prophet عَلَيْهِ ٱلسَّلَامُ, and to announce the deaths of Muslims and other righteous people." The second (MS ب) reads: "And go about announcing the deaths of the righteous." The wording in al-Zabīdī reads: "... [Hold to] the book of God and to the way of the righteous." Al-Zabīdī, *Itḥāf*, 8:126.

as he is alive in this world, and take [the fear of] its loss away from him. Make him content with the minimal allotment of this world, and whatever You give him of this world, make it easy for him to attain. Make him one of those who are grateful for all of Your favors that You bestow on him, and reward him on my behalf with the best of rewards."

Then [Uways] said, "I leave you in God's good care, Harim b. Ḥayyān. Peace and the mercy and blessings of God be on you. I will not see you after today—may God have mercy on you—when you search for me, for I despise fame. Solitude is more appealing to me, as I have many worries, and as long as I am alive, I am in extreme distress when among these people. So do not ask about me or search for me. But know that you are in my heart even if I never see you, nor you me. Remember me then and supplicate [to God] on my behalf, for I will remember you and will supplicate [to God] for you, God willing. [Now] leave this place so that I might leave it too."

I wanted to walk with him for a bit [lit., an hour], but he declined, so I parted ways with him. He began to weep, causing me to weep too. I began watching the back of his neck [as he walked away] until he entered a side street. Then, some time after that, I asked about him, but I never found anyone who could tell me anything about him. May God have mercy on him and forgive him.[25]

Such was the conduct of the children of the hereafter—those who turn away from this world. You have come to realize from what | precedes, in our elucidation of this world and from the conduct of the prophets and saints, that the extent of this world is everything that the sky shades and the earth carries, save what is for God عَزَّوَجَلَّ. The opposite of this world is the hereafter, which is everything [used] for the sake of God عَزَّوَجَلَّ, taken from this world to the extent needed, for the sake of [garnering enough] strength to obey God. That is not part of this world. 89

25 Ibn ʿAsākir, *Tārīkh madīnat Dimashq*, 9:431–434; Abū Nuʿaym, *Ḥilya*, 2:84–86. Cf. Ibn Saʿd al-Baṣrī, *Ṭabaqāt*, 8:285.

We will explain this by way of example. That is, the pilgrim, were he to vow that, while on the way to the pilgrimage, he would engage in nothing but the pilgrimage—that is, he would devote himself exclusively to it—and were he then to engage in securing his provisions, feeding his camel, sewing his water skin, and [doing] everything necessary for the pilgrimage, he would not have broken his vow, and he would not have been engaged in anything but the pilgrimage. Similarly, the body is the soul's vessel with which the span of one's life is traversed. Thus, maintaining the body with whatever knowledge and deeds preserve its strength for traveling the path—this is part of the hereafter and not part of this world.

Yes, if the intention is physical pleasure and [the enjoyment] of luxuries with any of these [worldly] means, then he has deviated from the hereafter, and it [should be] feared that his heart has become hardened.

Al-Ṭanāfisī said, "I was by the door of Banū Shayba of the Sacred Mosque of Mecca for seven continuous days, when on the eighth night, while I was between wakefulness and sleep, I heard a caller [say], 'Truly whoever takes from this world more than he needs, God will blind the eye of his heart!'"[26]

This then is for you an elucidation of the reality of this world. Know this and you will be well guided, if God تعالى so wills.

26 Cf. Ibn Ḥabīb, *ʿUqalāʾ al-majānīn*, 234–235 (no. 408), where a similar story is reported by Sumnūn b. Ḥamza "the Lover" (*al-Muḥibb*).

5

An Elucidation of the Essence of the World Itself and the Preoccupations that Overwhelm the Peoples' Endeavors Such That They Forget Themselves, Their Creator, and Their Beginning and Their End

90

KNOW that this world is a term to designate existing entities, a person's share of these, and the work he does in cultivating them. This is three matters, though one might think that this world is a term to designate only one of them, which is not the case.

As for the existing entities that this world as a term designates, they are the earth and everything that is on it. God تعالى has said, *Indeed, We have made that which is on the earth adornment for it that We may test them* [as to] *which of them is best in deed* [Q. 18:7]. For humans (Ādamīn) the earth is a spread-out space for resting, taking shelter, and settling. What is on it [the earth] is for them: clothing, food, drink, and mates.

What is on the earth is comprised of three divisions: minerals, plants, and animals.

As for plants, humans obtain these for nourishment and medicine.

As for minerals, humans obtain these for [making] tools and vessels (as in the case of copper and lead), or for currency (as in the case of gold and silver), or for other purposes.

As for animals, they are divided into [two]: people and beasts. In the case of beasts, one obtains their meat for food and [uses] their backs for riding, and ornamentation [to show off one's prestige]. In the case of people, a human might seek to possess people's bodies to use them for work or for their services (as in the case of male 91 slaves), or | to derive pleasure from them (as in the case of female slaves and women). A person seeks the hearts of other people to possess them [metaphorically] and instill awe and respect in them [for himself], and this is what is defined as "status," as the meaning of status is the possession of people's hearts.

These then are the entities that are designated this world. God تَعَالَىٰ gathered them together with His words, *Beautified for people is the love of that which they desire: of women and sons*, this is from the [category of] people, *heaped-up sums of gold and silver*, this is from the [category of] gems and minerals and indicates other things like pearls, precious stones, and other such things, *fine branded horses and cattle*, which are beasts and animals, *and tilled land* [Q. 3:14], and these are plants and crops.

These then are the entities of this world, except that they certainly have two connections to the servant.

[The first is] a connection with the heart. That is, his love for [a given entity], his share of it, and devoting his utmost concern to it such that his heart becomes like its slave or like the lover who is infatuated with this world. Included in this connection are all the qualities of the heart that are linked to this world, such as arrogance, spitefulness, envy, ostentation, repute, ill-thoughts [of others], love of praise, and love of competing and boasting. These constitute the inward portion of this world. The outer portion is the entities that we have already mentioned.

The second connection is with the body. That is, [the servant] occupies himself in the cultivation of these entities so that they might be useful to [increase] his fortunes or the fortunes of others. 92 This encompasses professions and trades that people engage in. |

People have forgotten about their souls, about their return [to God], and about their transition from this world merely on account of these two connections: the connection of the heart to love and the connection of the body to work. Were one to recognize his soul, recognize his Lord, and recognize the wisdom of this world and its mystery, he would know that these entities that we call the world were created only as feed for the beast that he is riding toward God تَعَالَىٰ.

By beast I mean the body, as it will not survive without food, drink, clothing, and shelter, just like the camel will not survive the path to the pilgrimage without feed, water, and saddle blankets.

The example of the servant in this world and [how] he loses sight of his soul and his purpose is like that of the pilgrim who stops at a waystation along the path and continues to feed his camel, attend to it, clean it, saddle it in colorful attire, bring it different types of grasses, cool its water with snow, until the caravan leaves him behind. Meanwhile, he is heedless of the pilgrimage, of the caravan's passing, and of his lingering in the wilderness (he and his camel [become] prey for predators). The insightful pilgrim is only concerned with his camel such that [he] enables it to cope with the trek. Thus he attends to it, while his heart is focused on the Kaʿba and the pilgrimage, and he pays his camel heed only to the extent that is necessary. Similarly, the insightful person on the journey to the hereafter occupies himself with attending to his body only in what is necessary, just as he enters the water closet only when necessary. There is no difference between putting food into the stomach and passing it out of the stomach in that both are bodily necessities. Whoever takes what he puts in his stomach as his highest ambition, his worth is the same as what passes out of it. And the stomach is what most frequently distracts people from God. Sustenance is a necessity, while shelter | and clothing are simpler. Were [people] to recognize the reason for their need of these things and limit their use of them, [their] preoccupations with this world would not absorb them so much. They are engrossed in them merely because of their ignorance of this world, of the wisdom [of its creation], and of their share of it. Rather, they are ignorant and heedless, while preoccupations with this world have inundated them, each [one] connected to the next, converging together with no end in sight. So they have become lost in [their] numerous preoccupations, and have forgotten their purpose. 93

[Here] we will mention details on the occupations of this world, how the need for them arises, and how people mistake their purposes. [We mention it] so that it becomes clear to you just how the occupations of this world have turned people away from God تَعَالَىٰ and have made them forget about the end result of their affairs. So, we say [the following].

Worldly occupations are all trades, professions, and work that you see people devoting themselves to. The reason that occupations are so numerous is that a person is compelled to [have] three things: sustenance, shelter, and clothing. Sustenance is for nourishment and survival; clothing is to protect against heat and cold; shelter is to protect against heat and cold and to protect one's family and wealth from the causes of destruction. God did not create sustenance, shelter, and clothing ready-made such that they have no need of human input. Yes, God did create it like that for beasts, as plants provide nourishment to an animal without [the need for] cooking, while heat and cold have no effect on its body,[27] and so it has no need to engage in construction. It finds contentment in the desert, while its clothing is its fur and hide, and so it has no need of [human] clothing. A person is not like this, and so the need arose for five

94 | occupations, which are the foundational industries and the first worldly occupations. They are farming, herding, hunting (*iqtināṣ*),[28] weaving, and construction.

Construction is for shelter. Weaving and what is related to it, [like] spinning thread and sewing, are for clothing. Farming is for food. The herding of cattle and horses is also for food and for transport. By hunting we mean the collection of what God created of game, minerals, vegetation, or firewood. So the farmer harvests plants; the herdsman safeguards his animals and breeds them; the hunter gathers what grows and reproduces by itself without human input. Similarly, he takes from the earth's minerals what was created in it with no human handiwork involved. This is what we mean by

27 Here, al-Ghazālī is not suggesting that animals do not sense heat and cold, pain, etc.; rather, he is referring to the idea that each animal was created to survive in the environment in which it lives and has no need of clothing in the way humans do [eds.].

28 The meaning of *iqtināṣ* (hunting) may also refer to foraging, but this meaning is not supported under the root ق - ن - ص by Wehr or Lane [eds.].

hunting, while a multitude of professions and occupations fall into this [category].

Furthermore, these professions require instruments and tools, as weaving, farming, construction, and hunting do. Tools can only be obtained from plants (namely timber), or from minerals (like iron, lead, and so forth), or from the hides of animals. Thus, the need arose for three additional types of professions; these are carpentry, metalwork, and leatherworking. These are the workers [who make] instruments. By carpenter we mean anyone who works with wood in whatever capacity. By metalworkers we mean anyone who works with precious minerals, including the coppersmith, the needle-maker, and others. [Here] our objective is to mention the broader categories [of professions]. As for specialized trades, they are too numerous [to mention]. By leatherworker we mean anyone who works with the hides of animals or parts thereof. These then are the foundational professions. | 95

Furthermore, a person was not created to live alone. Rather, he is compelled to gather together with others of his kind. This is for two reasons.

The first is his need to procreate to preserve the human species. This can only happen when the male and female come together and are intimate [with one another].

The second is [for humans] to cooperate in arranging the means of food and clothing production and in childrearing, for coming together will always result in a child, while the solitary individual cannot protect his child and arrange for the production of sustenance by himself. Moreover, it will not suffice for him to come together at home [alone] with his family and child. In fact, he would not be able to survive like this at all if a larger throng of people fails to come together for each member to undertake his profession. How could the solitary individual assume responsibility for farming by himself when he is in need of tools for it, and each tool requires a metalsmith or a carpenter, and his food requires a miller or a baker? Similarly, how could he singlehandedly produce clothing when he needs the cotton to be sown, and tools for weaving and sewing along with many other jobs? So for this it is impossible for a person to survive alone, and the need arises [for people] to gather together.

Furthermore, were [people] to gather together in an open desert, they would be harmed by the heat, cold, rain, and thieves, and they would be in need of fortified buildings and dwellings for each household individually, along with utensils and furnishings. The dwellings are to protect against the heat, cold, and rain and to protect against the harm of neighbors (in the form of thievery and so on). But a group of thieves from the outside may target the dwellings, and so the residents would need to help one another, cooperate with one another, 96 | and fortify themselves with walls that encompass all of the dwellings. Thus towns (*bilād*) came about for this necessity.[29]

Furthermore, whenever people come together in dwellings and towns and engage with one another, disputes arise between them. [Similarly], it occurs [with] the husband [who] has command and guardianship over his wife, and the parents [who have] guardianship over their child because he is weak and in need of someone to maintain him. Whenever guardianship takes place over a [person with] intellect (*ʿāqil*), it leads to dispute. This is in contrast to guardianship over beasts, as they lack the ability to dispute even if they are oppressed. As for the woman, she disputes with her husband, while the child disputes with his parents. This occurs in the home.

As for the townspeople, they too engage with one another [to meet] their needs, and they contend with one another over them. It they were left to their own devices, they would fight one another and perish. Likewise, the herdsmen and farmers come across herds, farmlands, and water that cannot satisfy all of their objectives, [so] it is inevitable that they will contend with one another [over these resources]. Moreover, some people may be incapable of farming or [another foundational type of] manufacturing because of blindness, illness, or old age (many different impediments arise). If [such a person] were left alone, he would perish. If [the task of] looking after him were entrusted to the group, they would turn their backs. If one of them were assigned the task with no rationale, he would not

29 *Bilād* (towns) could also designate villages depending on the context, or "any portion of the earth, or of land, comprehended within certain limits." See Lane, *An Arabic-English Lexicon*, 1:247 (s.v. ب - ل - د). Al-Zabīdī says that it is "any collection of people surrounded by a wall." Al-Zabīdī, *Itḥāf*, 8:131.

obey. Thus, owing to the necessity [engendered] by these occurrences that result from gathering together, other occupations came about. One of them is the profession of land-surveying, through which the earth's measures are known so that they can be divided fairly. Another is the profession of soldiering to guard the town with arms [lit., by the sword] and defend [them] against thieves. Another is the profession of governing and resolving disputes. Another is the need for jurisprudence (*fiqh*), which is knowledge of the law that should restrain people, while they are obliged to understand its boundaries so that fighting does not get out of hand. This is | knowledge of the boundaries of God تعالى as regards human interactions and their [legal] conditions. 97

These then are indispensable political matters that concern only those endowed with special attributes of knowledge, discernment, and guidance. Were [these specialists] to occupy themselves with these [professions], they would have no free time for any other profession. They need means to subsist on, while the townspeople are in need of them. For if the townspeople were to busy themselves in war against their enemies, for example, all industry would be suspended. Were the warriors and men-at-arms to occupy themselves with the [other] professions to search for sustenance, the town would lack sentries, and the people would suffer harm. Circumstances thus require that any neglected wealth that is ownerless (should it exist), be spent on their salaries and allowances. Or, the spoils of war are paid to [the specialists] if hostilities are with disbelievers. If [the soldiers] are men of religion and conscientiousness, they will be content with a small amount of [public] welfare money. If they want more, then circumstances inevitably require that the townspeople assist them, from their wealth, so that they [soldiers, etc.] provide security. The need then arises for a property tax (*kharāj*).[30]

Then, because of this need for a property tax, the need arises for other professions, as there is a need for someone to impose the tax fairly on farmers and those who possess wealth. These are the administrators. [There is also] a need for someone to collect it from them with civility. These are the tax collectors and assessors.

30 For a detailed legal treatment of the *kharāj* tax, see *al-Mawsūʿa al-fiqhiyya*, 19:51–91 (s.v. *kharāj*).

[There is also] the need for someone to gather [the taxes] together to safeguard them until the time for their disbursement. These are the treasurers. [There is also] the need for someone to disperse [the taxes] to the soldiers fairly. This is the soldiers' paymaster.

98 Were these jobs to be undertaken by a multitude of people who were not bound together in a coalition, the system would fail. | So the need arises for a king to manage them—a leader [or governor] (*amīr*), commanding obedience, who appoints a person to every job. For each person he chooses what best suits him. He has regard for justice when taking and dispersing property taxes, enlisting soldiers for war, distributing their weapons, determining the theaters of war, appointing the leader and general for each troop [of soldiers], in addition to other professions of governance. After the soldiers, who are the men-at-arms, and the king, who monitors them with a watchful eye and manages them, the need then arises for secretaries, treasurers, accountants, tax collectors, and administrators.

Then these people also require a livelihood, as they are unable to occupy themselves with [other] trades. Thus, the need arises for subsidiary financing in addition to the primary taxes. This is called "derivative taxes."

Accordingly, people [fall] into three professional groups.

The first [are] the farmers, herdsmen, and skilled craftsmen.

The second [are] the soldiers who protect them with arms.

The third [are] those who go back and forth between the [other] two groups to take and give [tax money]. These are the administrators, tax collectors, and the like.

So look how the matter began with the need for sustenance, shelter, and clothing, and where it ended up. Such are the affairs of this world: a door is not opened by one of them except that ten other doors are opened because of it. In this manner, [the affairs of this world] do not have a confined limit. They are like a bottomless abyss: whoever lands in a pit of them falls perpetually from one to the next and so on. |

99 These then are the trades and professions, though they can only be performed with wealth and tools. Wealth is a term to designate the entities of the earth and what [part] of it can benefit. Paramount

among these are nourishing [foods]. Next are the places in which a person takes shelter, namely homes. Next are the places in which [a person] works to [earn his] livelihood, like shops, markets, and farmlands. Next is clothing. Next are home furnishings and tools. Next are tools for the tools. An animal may be a tool, as is the case of the dog [that is] a tool for hunting, or the cow [that is] a tool for tilling, or the horse [that is] a tool for warfare. Then, the need for trade arises from all of this, as the farmer might reside in a village that lacks tools for farming, while the metalsmith and the carpenter reside in a village where agriculture is not possible. By necessity, the farmer needs them, and they need the farmer. Thus one of them needs to offer what he has to the other so that he might obtain his own objective from him. And this is by means of barter.

However, were the carpenter to seek nourishment from the farmer in exchange for his tool, for example, perhaps the farmer has no need of a tool at that time, so he does not sell [the tool] to him. And were the farmer [later] to seek the tool from the carpenter in exchange for food, perhaps [the carpenter] already has food at that time and so has no need of him. Their objectives are thus hindered, and so they would be forced to resort to a shop that stocks the tool of every profession, while its proprietor waits for those in need. They are obliged to [use] storerooms to stock the farmers' produce, so its proprietor can purchase them and wait for those in need. For this reason markets and storehouses emerged. Thus the farmer brings in his grain, and were he to find no one in need, he would sell it | to some of the merchants for a low price. Then they store it awhile and wait for those in need, hoping for a profit. The case for all merchandise and goods is similar. 100

Furthermore, it is inevitable that movement back and forth between the towns and villages will occur: people go back and forth buying food from the villages and tools from the towns. They transport them and make a living so that, because of them, the affairs of the townspeople are organized. As it may be that not every tool can be found in every town, and not every foodstuff can be found in every village, people are in need of one another and thus require transportation. And so merchants emerge who are in charge of transportation—the desire to acquire wealth inevitably motivates them. All day and night they tire themselves traveling to meet the needs of others, while their share in all of this is to acquire wealth that inevitably will be consumed by others, be it some highwayman or oppressive ruler. Even with their heedlessness and ignorance, God تَعَالَى created a system for the towns and a source of [public] welfare for His servants. In fact, it is because of heedlessness and base ambitions that all of the affairs of this world are organized. If people were intelligent and their ambitions lofty, they would deny themselves this world. If they were to do that, their livelihoods would be unfulfilled, and if this were to happen, they would all perish along with the ascetics too.

Furthermore, people are not capable of carrying and transporting these goods [on their backs or by themselves], and thus they need pack animals to carry them. The one providing the capital [for the enterprise] might not own an animal, and so an exchange takes place between him and the animal's owner, [and this is] called renting. Rental becomes another way of earning a living as well.

Furthermore, the need for appraisal arises on account of the merchandise.[31] For, [in the case of] the one who wants to | purchase food in exchange for an article of clothing—how would he know the amount of food that is its equivalent? Exchange occurs across all different types [of things], such as [an article of] clothing that is sold [in exchange] for food, or an animal [in exchange] for clothing. These are things that are not proportionate, and so there must be a fair judge to mediate between the two items and balance one against the other so that the correct measure of all goods is obtained.

101

Furthermore, there is a need for money that is durable, as [people's] need of it persists. The most durable of monies are metals, and so coins have been made from gold, silver, and copper.

Furthermore, circumstances require the minting, inscription, and valuation [of coins], and thus the need arises for the mint and for [money] changers.

In this [manner], occupations and jobs bring about one another, resulting in what you see.

---

31 Read *taqdīr* (appraisal) here for *naqdayn* (two currencies), as the former accords with the wording found in al-Zabīdī's version of the text and makes better sense in the context of the paragraph. Al-Zabīdī, *Itḥāf*, 8:134.

So these are people's occupations, which are their livelihoods.

Some of these trades can only be performed with some type of preliminary training and toil, while a person who neglects this in his youth cannot busy himself with it [as an adult]. Or, he is hindered by some obstacle, and so he remains incapable of earning a living because of his incapacity to [perform a] trade. Thus, he needs to consume what others have worked for. Two vile trades then arise from this [need]: thievery and begging; what links them is that they both consume the [fruits] of others' endeavors.

People are wary of thieves and beggars, and they safeguard their wealth from them. | So, [the thieves and beggars] must devote their intellects to devising all [sorts of] stratagems and ploys. As for the thieves, there is one who seeks out accomplices while possessing great prowess and strength. Then they get together, form a gang, and waylay [people], as is the case with the Bedouin and Kurds.[32] As for the weak ones, they take refuge in stratagems: by boring through or scaling [walls] when taking advantage of a chance moment of heedlessness, or by being a pickpocket or burglar, in addition to other types of thievery that occur in accordance with whatever originates in minds devoted to devising them.

102

As for the beggar, when he asks for the [fruits] of others' endeavors, he is told, "Toil and work like others do—why should you be idle?" Then he is not given anything. [Such people] are in need of a stratagem to extract wealth and prepare an excuse for themselves for their idleness, and so they trick [others] and use disability as an excuse. [This is done] in reality, like those who blind their children or themselves through the use of a stratagem so that they are excused on account of blindness and provided for. Or, [it is done] by pretending to be blind, paralyzed, insane, or ill, while demonstrating this through various types of stratagems and explaining that this is an affliction that struck [them] undeservedly so it can be used to garner pity.

Another group entreats by way of words and actions that the people marvel at, such that their hearts find joy in witnessing them.

32 Here al-Ghazālī's identification of Bedouin and Kurds simply indicates that these groups, at that time and in that context, may have been known to commit acts of banditry.

[These people] then let their hands relinquish a bit of money when they are in this state of wonderment. Later, when their wonderment subsides, they may regret [it], though this regret is of no use. These [words and actions] may be in the form of burlesque, | impersonation, sleight of hand, or slapstick. Or, it may be through strange poetry or rhymed prose [delivered] with a fine voice. Metered poetry has a greater effect on the soul, especially if it contains anything connected to sectarian zealotry,[33] such as poetry on the virtues of the Companions, or the virtues of the family of the Prophet (*ahl al-bayt*) رَضِوَٱللَّهُعَنْهُمْ. Or, it may be through whatever rouses the impulse for love among the impudent, like the craft of the drummers in the market. Or, it may be by handing over what appears to be a fair exchange but is not, like selling talismans or herbs that the seller pretends are medicinal, thereby deceiving the ignorant and children, like [what is done by] the astrologers who practice sortilege and fortune-telling. Included in this group are the admonishers who beg from the tops of the pulpits, assuming they lack useful knowledge to draw from, and their objective is to win over the hearts of the common folk and take their money. The types of begging exceed one or two thousand in number, and all of these are devised with deep thought for [the purpose of one's] livelihood.

103

So these are humanity's occupations and the labors to which they devote themselves, while the need for sustenance and clothing drags them into all of this. However, in the midst of it all, they forgot about their souls, about their purpose, about their transition [from this world], and about their return [to God]. So they have gone astray and have become lost. After the multitude of worldly preoccupations has troubled their weak intellects, corrupt fantasies come to them. Their paths divide and their opinions diverge on a number of standpoints.

One group was overcome by ignorance and heedlessness, and so their eyes are not opened to see the result of their affair. So they say, "The purpose [of life] is to live a [few] days in this world, and we exert ourselves so that we might earn our sustenance. Then we eat so we are strong [enough] to earn [a living]. Then we earn [a

33 *Taʿaṣṣubun*. The examples given in the passage here suggest that *madhāhib* refers to sectarian communities and not legal schools.

104

living] to eat." | Thus they eat to earn, and then earn to eat. This is the path of the farmers and the craftsmen and those who do not have luxuries in this world nor a foothold in the *dīn*: he toils in the day to eat at night and eats at night to toil in the day. This is like the way of the camels that draw water:[34] it is a journey that ceases only with death.

Another group claims to have comprehended the matter, namely that the purpose [of life] is not for a person to be miserable with work without enjoying luxury in this world. Rather, felicity is in satisfying his need of worldly desires, namely the desires of the stomach and the private parts. And so these people have forgotten about their souls and have set their ambitions on chasing women and gathering delectable foods. Then they eat like cattle do, thinking that if they partake of this then they have reached the pinnacle of happiness. All of this has diverted them from God تَعَالَىٰ and the last day.

Another group thought that felicity [lies] in the abundance of wealth and becoming rich through abundant treasures. So they lay awake at night and toil during the day to gather [it]. They tire [themselves] in travel all night and day, going back and forth in their onerous tasks, earning and gathering. They eat only the amount that is necessary out of greed and avarice so that [their wealth] does not diminish. This is their pleasure; this is their [sole] concern and enterprise until death overtakes them. Then [their wealth] is left behind under the ground, or someone seizes it and consumes it [in pursuit] of his desires and pleasures. The gatherer [suffers] | drudgery and anxieties, while the consumer [enjoys] its pleasure. Moreover, those who gather [wealth] see examples of this, but take no heed.

105

Another group thought that felicity is in having a good name, in [peoples'] tongues' uttering praise and commending [them] with exaggeration, and chivalry. So, they toil to earn their means of livelihood, and they restrict themselves in food and drink while spending all their wealth on fine garments and costly animals. They ornament the doors to [their] homes and anything else that people's eyes fall upon, so that it is said, "He is rich." Or, "He owns a fortune."

34 *Sayr al-sawānī* is "the course of the camels [that draw water]," which, according to an Arabic proverb, is a journey that never ends. See al-Maydānī, *Majmaʿ al-amthāl*, 1:42 (no. 1826).

They think that this is felicity, and so all night and all day their zeal is in attending to [outward] places people's eyes fall on.

Another group thought that felicity [lies] in status, in people's respect, and [leading] people through [their] humility and reverence. Thus, they set their ambitions on dragging people into submission by seeking out positions of sovereignty and taking over the tasks of government so that their authority over a group of people comes into effect by way of this. They believe that if their sovereignty expands and their subjects submit to them then they will have attained a felicity that is truly sublime—such is their ultimate pursuit. This is the foremost desire in the hearts of people who claim to be intelligent.[35] For such [people], the love of people's humbling themselves before them has distracted them from [their own] humility to God, from worship [of God], and from contemplation of their hereafter and their return [to God].

Beyond these groups are others that are too numerous to list: 106 they exceed seventy plus factions, | all of whom strayed and led others astray from the right path.[36] It is merely the need for food, clothing, and shelter that has dragged them into all of this, while they have forgotten what these three matters were intended for, and they have [lost sight of] the amount that suffices [of these three things]. The preliminary means to these things have dragged them along to their eventual consequences, and this has led them into abysses from which they can never ascend.

So, whoever knows the aspect of the need for these means and occupations and their ultimate goal would only undertake an occupation, trade, or work if he knows his goal and knows his share and allotment of it, and [knows] that his ultimate goal is to maintain his body with sustenance and clothing so that he does not perish.

In fact, if he were to follow the path of minimalism, [worldly] preoccupations would be driven from him, his heart would be freed, he would be overcome by remembrance of the hereafter, and his ambition would be set on preparing for it. If he were to exceed the

35 Other manuscripts, including those used by al-Zabīdī, replaced *al-mutaʿāqilūn* (those who claim to be intelligent) with *al-ghāfilūn* (the heedless). Al-Zabīdī, *Itḥāf*, 8:136.

36 Cf., inter alia, Q. 5:77: ...*A people who had gone astray before and misled many and have strayed from the soundnesss of the way.*

[minimum] amount that is necessary, his [worldly] preoccupations would multiply, evoke one another, and cascade without end. Then his worries would sidetrack him, and the one whose worries sidetrack him in the valleys of this world, God تَعَالَىٰ does not care which valley He destroys him in.[37]

So this is the state of the ones that are involved in preoccupations of this world.

One group was mindful of this, and so they turned away from this world. Then Satan grew envious of them, and without leaving them, he led them astray also in [the way] they turned away [from this world] until they became divided into [additional] groups. | 107

One group thought that this world is an abode of affliction and tribulation, while the hereafter is an abode of felicity for anyone who reaches it, whether he worshiped [God] in this world or did not worship. Thus, they decided that the correct course was to kill themselves to be liberated from the tribulation of this world.

A group of worshipers from India, in fact several groups, pursued this path. Thus, they fell on a fire and burned themselves to death while thinking that this is a liberation for them from the tribulations of this world.

Another group thought that killing [themselves] will not liberate [them], rather, it is first necessary to destroy one's human attributes and sever them completely from one's soul, [because] felicity is in cutting off one's desire and anger.

Thus, they turned to [spiritual] striving and were hard on themselves to the point that some of them perished from the severity of the discipline, the intellect of some of them was corrupted and they became insane, and some of them fell ill and were cut off from the path of worship, and some of them were unable to suppress their [human] characteristics in their entirety, so [they] came to think that what the law demanded was impossible and that the law was a deception with no basis to it. So he fell into apostasy.

37 Ibn Mājah relates a *ḥadīth* on the authority of Ibn Masʿūd رَضِيَ ٱللَّهُ عَنْهُ, who heard the Prophet say, "He who would consolidate his worries into worry for the hereafter, God suffices him in his worldly worries. He whose worries would sidetrack him into the concerns of this world, God does not care which of its valleys he is destroyed in." Ibn Mājah, *Sunan*, 1:95 (no. 257).

It seemed to some of them that all of this toil is for God, while God تَعَالَىٰ has no need of His servants' worship: a sinner's disobedience does not diminish Him, and a servant's worship does not increase Him. So they reverted to their desires, traveled the path of licentiousness, and rolled up the carpet on [lit., did away with] the law and its rulings. | 108

They claimed that [their reversion to their desires] is from the purity of their [conviction of God's] oneness, in that they believed that God has no need of His servants' worship.

Another group thought that the purpose behind [acts of] worship is [to undertake spiritual] striving so that the servant might attain the gnosis of God تَعَالَىٰ. Then, when gnosis results, he has "arrived," and after his arrival he has no need of any [further] expedients or stratagems.

So they abandoned [their] endeavors and worship, claiming that their station in the gnosis of God سُبْحَانَهُ rose beyond the point of being degraded by the obligations (*takālīf*) [of Islamic law]. These obligations are for the common folk.

Beyond these are other fallacious sects and appalling deviations that—reaching seventy plus factions—would take too long to enumerate.

Only one faction among them will be saved: the one that follows the way of the Messenger of God صَلَّى ٱللَّٰهُ عَلَيْهِ وَسَلَّمَ and his Companions.

[One must] not abandon this world in its entirety nor suppress desires in their entirety

As for this world, one takes from it the amount of provisions [necessary for the hereafter].

As for desires, one suppresses those that deviate from obedience to the law and to reason. Thus he does not follow every desire or abandon every desire, rather he follows an equitable [course] while not abandoning everything of this world nor seeking everything of this world.

In fact, he knows the purpose behind everything that God created of this world, and he maintains it in accordance with the limit [set by] this purpose. Thus he takes whatever sustenance is needed to strengthen his body for worship, whatever shelter is needed to protect him from | thieves, the heat, and the cold, and similarly, whatever clothing is needed. [He does this] so that when his heart is rid of physical distractions, he turns to God تَعَالَىٰ with true ardor, he busies himself with remembrance and reflection for the rest of his days, and he remains persistent in regulating [his] desires and monitoring them so that he does not exceed the limits of conscientiousness and piety. 109

He only knows the details of this by emulating the saved faction.

The saved faction is [that of] the Companions. For, when [the Prophet] صَلَّىٱللَّهُعَلَيْهِوَسَلَّمَ said, "Only one [of the seventy-three sects] will be saved," the [Companions] asked, "Oh Messenger of God! Who are they?" He replied, "Ahl al-Sunna wa-l-Jamāʿa." They asked, "Who are Ahl al-Sunna wa-l-Jamāʿa?" He replied, "[Those who follow] the way of my Companions and me."[38]

They were on the middle way and on the clear path that we have detailed.

Thus, they took nothing of this world for the sake of this world but rather for [the sake of] *dīn*. | 110

They did not practice monasticism nor relinquish this world in its entirety.

In their affairs there was neither renunciation nor immoderation, rather, their affairs were a balance between [the two], and that is equitable and moderate, between the two extremes. This is a most beloved matter to God تَعَالَىٰ, as was mentioned in places [above]. And God knows best.

---

38 Al-Tirmidhī relates a similar *ḥadīth* on the authority of ʿAbdallāh b. ʿAmr, رَضِيَٱللَّهُعَنْهُمَا who heard the Prophet صَلَّىٱللَّهُعَلَيْهِوَسَلَّمَ say, "What destroyed the children of Israel will surely destroy my community in the exact same manner, to the extent that, were one of them to have had public intercourse with his mother, there would be someone from my community who would do the same. The children of Israel split into seventy-two sects (*milla*), while my community will split into seventy-three. All of them will be in the fire except one." They asked, "Oh Messenger of God! Which one is that?" He replied, "Those who follow the way of my Companions and me." Al-Tirmidhī, *Sunan*, 5:26 (no. 2641). In a similar *ḥadīth* related by Abū Dāwūd, Muʿāwiya رَضِيَٱللَّهُعَنْهُ reports that the Prophet identified "the majority faction" (*al-jamāʿa*) as the one sect that will enter heaven. Abū Dāwūd, *Sunan*, 5:7–8 (no. 4597). For an extensive discussion of the faction that will be saved, see al-Zabīdī, *Itḥāf*, 8:140–141.

Praise be to God in the beginning and in the end, and may God's blessings and peace be on our master Muḥammad and his family and Companions.

So concludes the *Book of the Censure of This World*, being the Sixth Book in the Quarter of Perils of *The Revival of the Religious Sciences*. May God's blessings be on our master Muḥammad, the chosen Arabian Prophet, on his family, who are good and pure, and on his Companions, one and all. Following it is the *Book of the Censure of Greed and [the Love of] Wealth.*

Bibliography

Works in Western Languages

Khalidi, Tarif. *The Muslim Jesus: Sayings and Stories in Islamic Literature*. Cambridge, MA: Harvard University Press, 2001.

Lane, E. W. *An Arabic-English Lexicon*. 8 vols. Beirut: Librairie du Liban, 1968.

Stoetzer, Wilhelmus. "Prosody (*ʿarūḍ*)." In *The Routledge Encyclopedia of Arabic Literature*. Edited by Julie Scott Meisami and Paul Starkey, 619–622. London and New York: Routledge, 2010.

Works in Arabic

ʿAbbās, Iḥsān (ed.). *Shiʿr al-khawārij*. Beirut: Dār al-Thaqāfa, 1974.

al-Ābī, Manṣūr b. al-Ḥusayn. *Nathr al-durr*. Edited by Muḥammad ʿAli Qurna and ʿAlī Muḥammad al-Bajāwī. 7 vols. Cairo: al-Hayʾa al-Miṣriyya al-ʿĀmma li-l-Kitāb, 1980–.

Abū l-ʿAtāhiyya, Ismāʿīl b. al-Qāsim. *Abū l-ʿAtāhiyya: ashʿāruhu wa-akhbāruhu*. Edited by Shukrī Fayṣal. Damascus: Maṭbaʿat Jāmiʿat Dimashq, 1965.

Abū Dāwūd al-Sijistānī, Sulaymān b. Ashʿath. *Sunan Abī Dāwūd*. Edited by ʿIzzat ʿAbīd al-Daʿās and ʿĀdil al-Sayyid. 5 vols. Beirut: Dār Ibn Ḥazm, 1997.

Abū Nuʿaym al-Iṣbahānī, Aḥmad b. ʿAbdallāh. *Ḥilyat al-awliyāʾ wa-ṭabaqāt al-aṣfiyāʾ*. 11 vols. Cairo: Maṭbaʿāt al-Saʿāda wa-l-Khānjī, 1357/1938; repr. Beirut: Dār al-Kitāb al-ʿArabī, 1987.

Abū Nuwās, al-Ḥasan b. Hāniʾ. *Dīwān Abī Nuwās bi-riwāyat al-Ṣūlī*. Edited by Bahjat ʿAbd al-Ghafūr al-Ḥadīthī. Abu Dhabi: Abu Dhabi Authority for Culture and Heritage, 2010.

Abū Ṭālib al-Makkī, Muḥammad b. ʿAlī. *Qūt al-qulūb*. Edited by Muḥammad al-Zaharī al-Ghumarāwī. 2 vols. Cairo: al-Maṭbaʿa al-Maymaniyya, 1310/1893; repr. Beirut: Dār Ṣādir/Dār al-Fikr, 2004.

ʿAlī b. Abī Ṭālib. *Dīwān al-Imām ʿAlī (Anwār al-ʿuqūl min ashʿār waṣiyy al-rasūl)*. Edited by Kāmil Salmān al-Jubūrī. Beirut: Dār al-Maḥajja al-Bayḍāʾ, 1999.

al-ʿĀmirī, Labīd b. Rabīʿa. *Dīwān Labīd b. Rabīʿa al-ʿĀmirī*. Beirut: Dār Ṣādir, 1966.

al-ʿAsqalānī, Aḥmad Ibn Ḥajar. *al-Talkhīṣ al-ḥabīr*. Edited by Muḥammad al-Thānī Mūsā. 7 vols. Riyadh: Dār Aḍwāʾ al-Salaf, 2007.

al-Bāhilī, Muḥammad b. Ḥāzim. *Dīwān al-Bāhilī*. Edited by Muḥammad Khayr al-Biqāʿī. Damascus: Dār Qutayba, 1982.

al-Bayhaqī, Aḥmad b. al-Ḥusayn. *al-Jāmiʿ li-shuʿab al-īmān*. Edited by ʿAbd al-ʿAlī ʿAbd al-Ḥamīd Ḥāmid. 14 vols. Riyadh: Maktabat al-Rushd, 2004.

al-Bayhaqī, Aḥmad b. al-Ḥusayn. *Kitāb al-zuhd al-kabīr*. Edited by ʿĀmir Aḥmad Ḥaydar. Beirut: Dār al-Jinān, 1987.

al-Bazzār, Abū Bakr b. Aḥmad b. ʿAmr. *al-Baḥr al-zakhkhār* (known as *Musnad al-Bazzār*). Edited by Maḥfūẓ al-Raḥmān Zaynallāh. 20 vols. Medina: Maktabat al-ʿUlūm wa-l-Ḥikam, 1988.

al-Bukhārī, Muḥammad b. Ismāʿīl b. Ibrāhīm. *Ṣaḥīḥ al-Bukhārī*. 9 vols. Būlāq, 1311–1313; repr. Beirut: Dār Ṭawq al-Najāt, 1422/2001.

al-Daylamī, Shīrawayh b. Shahdār. *al-Firdaws bi-maʾthūr al-khiṭāb* (= *Musnad al-firdaws*). Edited by Saʿīd b. Basyūnī Zaghlūl. 6 vols. Beirut: Dār al-Kutub al-ʿIlmiyya, 1986.

al-Dhahabī, Muḥammad b. Aḥmad. *Siyar aʿlām al-nubalāʾ*. Edited by Shuʿayb al-Arnāʾūṭ, et al. 28 vols. Beirut: Muʾassasat al-Risāla, 1996.

al-Dīnawarī, Aḥmad b. Marwān b. Muḥammad. *al-Majālisa wa-jawāhir al-ʿilm*. Beirut: Dār Ibn Ḥazm, 2002.

al-Ghazālī, Abū Ḥāmid Muḥammad b. Muḥammad. *al-Munqidh min al-ḍalāl*. Edited by Maḥmūd Bījū. Damascus: Maṭbaʿat al-Ṣabāḥ, 1993.

al-Ḥākim al-Nīsābūrī, Muḥammad b. ʿAbdallāh. *al-Mustadrak ʿalā l-Ṣaḥīḥayn*. 5 vols. Hyderabad: Dāʾirat al-Maʿārif al-Niẓāmiyya, 1335/1917; repr. Beirut: Dār al-Maʿrifa, n.d.

al-ʿIbādī, ʿAdī b. Zayd. *Dīwān Adī b. Zayd al-ʿIbādī*. Edited by Muḥammad Jabbār al-Muʿaybid. Baghdad: Sharikat Dār al-Jumhūriyya, 1965.

Ibn ʿAbd al-Barr, Yūsuf b. ʿAbdallāh al-Nimrī. *Bahjat al-majālis*. Edited by Muḥammad Mursī al-Khūrī. 3 vols. Beirut: Dār al-Kutub al-ʿIlmiyya, 1981.

Ibn Abī l-Dunyā, ʿAbdallāh b. Muḥammad al-Qurashī. *Dhamm al-dunyā*. Edited by Muḥammad ʿAbd al-Qādir Aḥmad ʿAṭā. Beirut: Muʾassasat al-Kutub al-Thaqāfiyya, 1993.

Ibn Abī l-Dunyā, ʿAbdallāh b. Muḥammad al-Qurashī. *al-ʿIyyāl*. Edited by Najm ʿAbd al-Raḥmān Khalaf. Cairo: Dār al-Wafāʾ, 1997.

Ibn Abī l-Dunyā, ʿAbdallāh b. Muḥammad al-Qurashī. *Qiṣar al-amal*. Edited by Muḥammad Khayr Ramaḍān Yūsuf. Beirut: Dār Ibn Ḥazm, 1995.

Ibn Abī l-Dunyā, ʿAbdallāh b. Muḥammad al-Qurashī. *al-Tawāḍuʿ wa-l-khumūl*. Edited by Luṭfī Muḥammad al-Ṣaghīr. Cairo: Dār al-Iʿtiṣām, n.d.

Ibn Abī l-Dunyā, ʿAbdallāh b. Muḥammad al-Qurashī. *Kitāb al-zuhd*. Damascus and Beirut: Dār Ibn Kathīr, 1999.

Ibn Abī l-Ḥadīd, ʿAbd al-Ḥamīd b. Hibatallāh. *Sharḥ Nahj al-balāgha*. Edited by Muḥammad Abū l-Faḍl Ibrāhīm. 20 vols. Qom: Muʾassasat Ismāʿīliyān, 1963.

Ibn Abī Ḥaṣīna, al-Ḥasan b. ʿAbdallāh. *Dīwān Ibn Abī Ḥaṣīna*. Edited by Muḥammad Asʿad Ṭalas. 2 vols. Beirut: Dār Ṣādir, 1999.

Ibn Abī Shayba, ʿAbdallāh b. Muḥammad. *al-Muṣannaf*. Edited by Muḥammad ʿAwwāma. 26 vols. Jedda: Dār al-Qibla, 2006.

Ibn al-Aʿrābī, Aḥmad b. Muḥammad b. Ziyād. *al-Muʿjam*. Edited by ʿAbd al-Muḥsin b. Ibrāhīm b. Aḥmad al-Ḥusaynī. Riyadh: Dār Ibn al-Jawzī, 1997.

Ibn ʿAsākir, ʿAlī b. al-Ḥasan. *Tārīkh madīnat Dimashq*. Edited by Muḥibb al-Dīn ʿUmar b. Gharāma al-ʿUmrāwī. 80 vols. Beirut: Dār al-Fikr, 1995.

Ibn Bālabān al-Fārisī, ʿAlī. *al-Iḥsān fī taqrīb Ibn Ḥibbān (al-Musnad al-ṣaḥīḥ ʿalā l-taqāsīm wa-l-anwāʿ min ghayr wujūd qaṭaʿ fī sanadihā wa-lā thubūt jarḥ fī nāqilīhā)*. Edited by Shuʿayb al-Arnāʾūṭ. 18 vols. Beirut: Muʾassasat al-Risāla, 1997.

Ibn Ḥabīb, al-Ḥasan b. Muḥammad. *ʿUqalāʾ al-majānīn*. Edited by ʿUmar al-Asʿad. Beirut: Dār al-Nafāʾis, 1987.

Ibn Ḥanbal, Aḥmad. *Musnad al-Imām Aḥmad b. Ḥanbal*. Edited by Shuʿayb al-Arnāʾūṭ. 50 vols. Beirut: Muʾassasat al-Risāla, 1995.

Ibn Ḥanbal, Aḥmad. *al-Zuhd*. Edited by Muḥammad ʿAbd al-Salām Shāhīn. Beirut: Dār al-Kutub al-ʿIlmiyya, 1999.

Ibn al-Jawzī, ʿAbd al-Raḥmān b. ʿAlī. *al-Mudhish*. Edited by ʿAbd al-Karīm Muḥammad Munīr Tattān and Khaldūn ʿAbd al-ʿAzīz Makhlūṭa. 2 vols. Damascus: Dār al-Qalam, 2014.

Ibn Mājah, Muḥammad b. Yazīd. *Sunan Ibn Mājah*. Edited by Muḥammad Fuʾād ʿAbd al-Bāqī. 2 vols. Cairo: Dār Iḥyāʾ al-Kutub al-ʿArabiyya, 1954.

Ibn Manẓūr, Muḥammad b. Mukarram. *Mukhtaṣar Tārīkh Dimashq li-Ibn ʿAsākir*. Edited by Rūḥiyya al-Naḥḥās, Riyāḍ ʿAbd al-Ḥamīd Murād, and Muḥammad Muṭīʿ al-Ḥāfiẓ. 31 vols. Beirut and Damascus: Dār al-Fikr, 1984.

Ibn al-Mubārak, ʿAbdallāh. *Dīwān al-Imām*. Edited by Mujāhid Muṣṭafā Bahjat. Mansoura: Dār al-Wafāʾ, 1992.

Ibn al-Mubārak, ʿAbdallāh. *al-Zuhd wa-l-raqāʾiq*. Edited by Ḥabīb al-Raḥmān al-Aʿẓamī. Beirut: Dār al-Kutub al-ʿIlmiyya, 2004.

Ibn Qutayba al-Dīnawarī, ʿAbdallāh b. Muslim. ʿUyūn al-akhbār. 4 vols. Cairo: Dār al-Kutub al-Miṣriyya, 1930.

Ibn Saʿd al-Baṣrī, Muḥammad. *al-Ṭabaqāt al-kabīr*. Edited by ʿAlī Muḥammad ʿUmar. 11 vols. Cairo: Maktabat al-Khānjī, 2001.

al-Ishbīlī, ʿAbd al-Ḥaqq. *al-ʿĀqiba fī dhikr al-mawt wa-l-ākhira*. Edited by Khiḍr Muḥammad Khiḍr. Kuwait: Maktabat al-Aqṣā, 1986.

al-Kharāʾiṭī, Muḥammad b. Jaʿfar. *Iʿtilāl al-qulūb*. Edited by Ḥamdī al-Dimirdāsh. 2 vols. Riyadh: Maktabat Nizār Muṣṭafā al-Bāz, 2000.

al-Khaṭīb al-Baghdādī, Aḥmad b. ʿAlī. *Tārīkh Baghdād*. Edited by Muṣṭafā ʿAbd al-Qādir ʿAṭā. 24 vols. Beirut: Dār al-Kutub al-ʿIlmiyya, 1997.

al-Marwazī, Nuʿaym b. Ḥammād al-Khuzāʿī. *Kitāb al-Fitan*. Edited by Majdī b. Manṣūr b. Sayyid al-Shūrā. Beirut: Dār al-Kutub al-ʿIlmiyya, 1997.

al-Mawsūʿa al-fiqhiyya. 45 vols. Kuwait: Kuwaiti Ministry of Awqāf and Islamic Affairs, 1997.

al-Maydānī, Aḥmad b. Muḥammad. *Majmaʿ al-amthāl*. Edited by Muḥammad Muḥyī l-Dīn ʿAbd al-Ḥamīd. 2 vols. Beirut: Dār al-Maʿrifa, 1953.

Muslim b. al-Ḥajjāj al-Qushayrī al-Nīsābūrī. *al-Jāmiʿ al-ṣaḥīḥ*. Edited by Muḥammad Fuʾād ʿAbd al-Bāqī. 5 vols. Cairo and Beirut: Dār Iḥyāʾ al-Kutub al-ʿArabiyya, 1954.

al-Nasāʾī, Aḥmad b. Shuʿayb. *Sunan al-Nasāʾī*. 9 vols. Cairo: al-Maṭbaʿa al-Maymaniyya, 1312/1894; repr. Beirut: Dār al-Kitāb al-ʿArabī, n.d.

al-Qushayrī, ʿAbd al-Karīm. *al-Risāla al-Qushayriyya*. Edited by ʿAbd al-Ḥalīm Maḥmūd and Maḥmūd b. al-Sharīf. Cairo: Dār al-Shaʿb, 1989.

al-Rāghib al-Iṣfahānī, al-Ḥusayn b. Muḥammad. *al-Dharīʿa ilā makārim al-sharīʿa*. Edited by Abū l-Yazīd Abū Zayd al-ʿAjamī. Cairo: Dār al-Salām, 2007.

al-Ṭabarānī, Sulaymān b. Aḥmad. *al-Aḥādīth al-ṭawāl*. Edited by Ḥamdī ʿAbd al-Majīd al-Salafī. Beirut: al-Maktab al-Islāmī, 1998.

al-Ṭabarānī, Sulaymān b. Aḥmad. *al-Muʿjam al-awsaṭ*. 10 vols. Cairo: Dār al-Ḥaramayn, 1995.

al-Ṭabarānī, Sulaymān b. Aḥmad. *al-Muʿjam al-kabīr*. Edited by Ḥamdī ʿAbd al-Majīd al-Salafī. 25 vols. Beirut: Dār Iḥyāʾ al-Turāth al-ʿArabī, n.d.

al-Thaʿālibī, ʿAbd al-Malik b. Muḥammad Abū Manṣūr. *al-Tamthīl wa-l-muḥāḍara*. Edited by ʿAbd al-Fattāḥ Muḥammad al-Ḥulw. Cairo: al-Dār al-ʿArabiyya li-l-Kitāb, 1983.

al-Tirmidhī, Muḥammad b. ʿĪsā. *Sunan al-Tirmidhī = al-Jāmiʿ al-ṣaḥīḥ*. Edited by Aḥmad Shākir, Muḥammad Fuʾād ʿAbd al-Bāqī, and Ibrāhīm ʿAṭwa ʿAwaḍ. 5 vols. Beirut: Dār Iḥyāʾ al-Turāth al-ʿArabī, n.d. [reprint of Cairo, 1938 edition].

al-Warrāq, Maḥmūd. *Dīwān Maḥmūd al-Warrāq*. Edited by Walīd al-Qaṣāb. Damascus: Muʾassasat al-Funūn, 1991.

al-Zabīdī, Muḥammad Murtaḍā. *Itḥāf al-sāda al-muttaqīn bi-sharḥ Iḥyāʾ ʿulūm al-dīn*. 10 vols. Cairo: al-Maṭbaʿa al-Maymaniyya, 1311/1894.

al-Zamakhsharī, Maḥmūd b. ʿUmar. *Rabīʿ al-abrār wa-nuṣūṣ al-akhbār*. Edited by Salīm al-Nuʿaymī. 5 vols. Tehran: Dār al-Dhakhāʾir, 1990.

Index of Qurʾānic Verses

Index of *Ḥadīth*

Index of People and Places

Subject Index

About the Translator

Matthew Ingalls is Associate Professor of Middle Eastern Studies and Chair of the Department of International and Middle Eastern Studies at the American University in Dubai. He completed a Master's degree in Arabic Studies at the American University in Cairo and received his doctorate from Yale University's Department of Religious Studies in 2011. Before joining the AUD faculty in the fall of 2016, Matthew taught Islamic Studies and Religious Studies at the University of Puget Sound in Tacoma, Washington. He has published articles in the study of Sufism and Islamic law during the later Islamic Middle Period (1250–1500), while his current research examines pre-modern Muslim commentary works and their role in intellectual change. His academic monograph *The Anonymity of a Commentator: Zakariyya al-Anṣarī and the Rhetoric of Muslim Commentaries* was published by the State University of New York Press in September 2021.

This publication was made possible through the generous
support of Ikbal and Ercument Tokat and SufiCorner.
May God reward them and their family.